Immanent Visitor

Immanent Visitor

Selected Poems of Jaime Saenz

A BILINGUAL EDITION

TRANSLATED FROM THE SPANISH BY

Kent Johnson and Forrest Gander

UNIVERSITY OF CALIFORNIA PRESS

BERKELEY   LOS ANGELES   LONDON

University of California Press
Berkeley and Los Angeles, California

University of California Press, Ltd.
London, England

Poems in English translation © 2002 by The Regents
of the University of California

Poems in original Spanish © 2002 by the Estate of Jaime Saenz

All photographs reproduced in this book appear courtesy of the
Estate of Jaime Saenz. The photographers are unknown.

Library of Congress Cataloging-in-Publication Data

Sáenz, Jaime, 1921–1986.
[Visitante profundo. English and Spanish]
    Immanent visitor : selected poems of Jaime Saenz / translated
from the Spanish by Kent Johnson and Forrest Gander.
        p.   cm.
    ISBN 0-520-23047-7 (cloth : alk. paper)—
    ISBN 0-520-23048-5 (paper : alk. paper)
    I. Saenz, Jaime.   I. Johnson, Kent; Gander, Forrest.
II. Title.
PQ7819.S22 V5   2002
861'.64—dc21   2002074210
                                                      CIP

Manufactured in the United States of America

11   10   09   08   07   06   05   04   03   02
10   9   8   7   6   5   4   3   2   1

The paper used in this publication meets the minimum require-
ments of ANSI/NISO Z39.48-1992 (R 1997) *(Permanence of
Paper)*. ∞

Contents

POEMS IN THE
ORIGINAL SPANISH

Acknowledgments

The translators are immensely grateful to the late
Dr. Arturo Orias, and to Elva Gonzalez de Morales,
executors of the Jaime Saenz estate. Special grati-
tude, as well, to Ximena Morales, Gisela Morales,
and Tina Orias for their generous assistance in fa-
cilitating communications and for their help with the
securing and scanning of visual materials included
in this book.

Kent Johnson would like to thank Highland
Community College for granting a sabbatical leave
during the 1998 and 1999 academic year, awarded
for the purposes of undertaking this translation proj-
ect, and to acknowledge and thank his friends and
colleagues at Highland—Andy Dvorak, Kim Goud-
reau, and Carol Redmore—for their inspiring sup-
port and encouragement. Above all, thanks to Debi,
Brooks, and Aaron for their patience, counsel, and
love.

Forrest Gander would like to thank some of those
writers-and-translators whose works and friendships
have both been important to him: Norma Cole, Peter
Cole, Arthur Sze, Cole Swensen, Nathaniel Tarn,
Donald Revell, Robert Hass, Keith and Rosmarie
Waldrop, Monica de la Torre, and Carolyn Forché,
as well as the writing community in Providence,

where translation and poetry have flourished and nourished him.

Kent and Forrest would like to jointly thank Eliot Weinberger and Cecilia Vicuña for their support of this project and for their own inspiring work.

Katherine Hyde-Flanagan translated the afterword on short notice. Norbert Francis of Northern Arizona University and Cole Heinowitz of Brown University offered suggestions and translated critical materials by Leonardo García-Pabón, which we finally chose not to use in this particular volume but which served to inspire some of our introductory remarks. We are thankful to each of them, and to Elena del Rio Parra, who typed many of the poems in Spanish onto disk.

We are grateful, too, to the editors who published sections of these translations first: Cecilia Vicuña in her anthology of Latin American poetry (forthcoming from Oxford University Press), Suzan Sherman at *Bomb Magazine*, John Tranter at *Jacket* (www. jacket.zip.com.au), Rebecca Woolf at *Fence*, and Garrett Kalleberg and Leonard Schwartz at *The Transcendental Friend* (www.morningred.com/friend), and Lindsay Hill and Paul Taylor at *Facture*.

The drawing of skulls on page 4 is by Jaime Saenz. The photographs of Saenz were taken by unidentified photographers.

Finally, but not in the spirit of finality, the translators acknowledge the poet and critic Leonardo García-Pabón, without whose patient advice this project would not have come to fruition. He was a friend and colleague of Jaime Saenz, and he now works with generous energy and eloquence to bring this great poet's work to the attention of the world. We dedicate this translation to him.

By Way of Introduction

Poet and novelist Jaime Saenz (1921–1986) lived his whole life in La Paz, Bolivia, seldom venturing beyond that thin-aired and scarcely believable city. His life was defined by an intense experience of alcoholism, a struggle, eventually lost, that was wedded to what Leonardo García-Pabón, one of the leading scholars on Saenz's work, has called a "monastic" dedication to writing.[1] There was in his persona a near-total rejection of the social niceties and conventions of polite society. Quite to the letter, in fact, Saenz embodied, for much of his adult life, the late-Romantic idea of the *poète maudit*—apocalyptic and occult in his politics, habituous of slum taverns, unashamedly bisexual, insistently nocturnal in his artistic affairs, secretive in his leadership of a select group of writers—and he became, in the staid and tradition-bound circles of Bolivian high culture, the ongoing subject of rumor and gossip.

For a number of years in his youth, Saenz worked as a cultural liaison with the U.S. Information Ser-

1. Saenz succeeded in staying sober, with a few brief, notorious setbacks, for almost twenty years (the period of his greatest output). He succumbed again to drink in the year leading up to his death. His final book of poetry, *La noche* (The night) is a harrowing and moving account of alcoholic experience.

vice. Later he worked on and off as a journalist and professor and maintained important friendships with painters, composers, and intellectuals. But he essentially lived in poverty all his life. He wrote by night and drank excessively, and his public behavior was sometimes scandalous. In the 1960s and 1970s, while his great Bolivian contemporary, Oscar Cerruto, was gaining a reputation for poetry of formal and psychological nuance, and as the global reach of postmodernism was beginning to rush literature into radical new forms, Saenz, stubbornly mystical and baroque, was on his own. His work was certainly innovative, absorbing the fantastic, the psychological, and the symbolic. But it wasn't formally radical enough to situate him among the international avant-garde; it wasn't politically specific enough to find favor with the ascendant literary left, and it was too weird to ride into popularity on the coattails of writers like Cortázar and Vargas Llosa during the Latin American boom of the 1970s. The artists and writers of his generation recognized him as a major force, but until Blanca Wiethüchter wrote a tide-turning book-length study of his poetry, late in his career, Saenz's work was published to a general critical silence. Today, he is widely regarded as Bolivia's most original and visionary poet. While his brilliant and courageous fiction still remains little known outside his own nation, his poetry has recently been translated and published in a number of European countries and is gaining increasing attention there and throughout Latin America as among the most compelling and idiosyncratic of the Spanish-speaking world.[2]

A propulsive, energetic rhythmical drive and an aching emotional expressiveness hold the poems of Jaime Saenz together, even as they seem to burst

---

2. Saenz's published novels are *Felipe Delgado* (Felipe Delgado, 1979) and *Los papeles de Narciso Lima-Acha* (The papers of Narciso Lima-Acha, 1991). The latter, originally written in the 1960s, and recognized as one of Bolivia's greatest works of fiction, is also one of Latin America's first openly gay novels. Saenz's poetry includes the following books: *El escalpelo* (The scalpel, 1955), *Muerte por el tacto* (Death by feel, 1957), *Aniversario de una visión* (Anniversary of a vision, 1960), *Visitante profundo* (Immanent visitor, 1964), *El frío* (The cold, 1967), *Al pasar un cometa* (As the comet passes, 1982), *Recorrer esta distancia* (To cross this distance, 1973), *Bruckner* (Bruckner, 1978), *Las tinieblas* (The darknesses, 1978), and *La noche* (The night, 1984). *El escalpelo*, *Muerte por el tacto*, *Aniversario de una visión*, *Visitante profundo*, *El frío*, and *Recorrer esta distancia* have been collected into a single volume as *Obra poética* (Poetic work, La Paz: Biblioteca del Sesquicentenario de la Republica, 1975). The following are among a growing body of critical essays in Spanish on the poetry of Saenz: Blanca Wiethüchter, "Estructuras de lo imaginario en la obra poética de Jaime Saenz" (Structures of the imaginary in the poetic work of Jaime Saenz), a book-length essay presented as critical Appendix to *Obra poética* (ed. cit.); Luis H. Antezana, "La obra poética de Jaime Saenz" (The poetic work of Jaime Saenz) in *Hombres y letras* (Men and letters), no. 1 (1979); Maria Julia de Ruschi Crespo, "El ropaje y la música: Un ensayo sobre Jaime Saenz" (Robes and music: An essay on Jaime Saenz) in *Usos de la imaginación* (Uses of the imagination, Buenos Aires, 1984), and Leonardo García-Pabón, "Escribir antes y después de la muerte/Sobre la obra poética de Jaime Saenz" (Writing before and after death/On the poetic work of Jaime Saenz) in *Revista Iberoamericana* 134 (1986): 285–89).

from the syntactical conventions of familiar language practices. Like most of the important modernist poets, Saenz has been called "difficult," but the poems are not difficult to feel. In long lines, in odes that name desire, with Whitmanesque anaphora, in exclamations and repetitions, Saenz addresses the reader, the beloved, and death in one extended lyrical gesture. The poems are brazenly affecting. Their semantic difficulty lies, chiefly, in the odd heterogeneity of their formal and tonal structures, which careen, unabashedly, between modes and moods: now archly lyrical, now arcanely symbolic, now man-in-the-street colloquial, now trancelike in pronominal scramblings at the seeming edge of glossolalia.

For a poet continually astounded both by the fact of being alive and by the obdurate nearness of death, a poet surrounded both by the jubilant exaltation of living and by the poverty and despair of a degraded world, paradox weaves together the nature of experience. In Saenz's poems the sacred word and silence, quotidian sensibility and psychic ecstasy, a spectral "I" and "you" are always interacting in a dialectic that surges toward the potential for perception and language to ignite revelation. It is important, and here also paradoxical, that such revelation for Saenz lay hidden and expectant in death. But far from being the mere consequence or residue of linear time, death's phenomenal expression is, for the poet, more like a capsuled configuration of space, the eruption of a wormhole, so to say, that beckons and leads—though the living can hardly yet follow—into an adjoining dimension of intensified and unbounded presence. To Saenz, death's material, bodily manifestation is the still-wet shore between realms, a wavelike arrival and slow drawing back, the whispered lapping of an unfathomable totality he calls "real life." And it is this fundamental conjoining of existences that is the master conceit of his great poem *To Cross This Distance* (*Recorrer esta distancia*, 1973). Death's immanence as the indivisible and necessary ground of life and love haunts all of Saenz's work and connects it, significantly, to the spiritual world of the Indians in Bolivia.

In this sense, if Saenz's poetry can be said to exist under the sign of the hermetic, it is a hermeticism that is not so much in the typical function of language experiment and avant-garde social critique as it is in service of a visionary impulse unapologetic in its romanticism and in its identification with indigenous Bolivian cultures. By emphasizing nonlinear time, suspended states of knowing, and mystical realms of death and by conflating memory, death, linguistics, and sensual experience into any given moment of experience, Saenz connects his poetry to the visionary world of the Kallawaya, Aymara, and Quechua, with which he was fascinated. The influence of Aymara culture can be seen as well in his talismanic words, his symmetrical grammatical structures, and his affirmation of conceptual opposites. At times, though, in the way he transposes profound feeling into a language of paradox, Saenz can sound, to ears tuned to Western literature, very much like the Petrarch of *Sonnet 118:*

> Now here I am, alas, and wish I were elsewhere,
> and wish I wished more, but wish no more,
> and, by being unable to do more, do all I can

Never merely plumping a naive Romanticism, where words "come after" intense feeling and "express" it, Saenz's language emphatically constitutes the initiatory field. At once numinous and material, then, his poetry is both bottomless riddle and the very means for bridging and canceling the central antinomies— self and other, mind and world, indigenous and colonial, the living and the dead—that fuel the thematic of his artistic quest.

It is in this sense that his work, in a deeply multiethnic and multilingual Bolivia, constitutes much more than an instance of bohemian or elitist aestheticism. As García-Pabón has pointed out, its powerful clearing of a free zone of expression at the center of "high culture" has reinforced and extended the resistance of marginalized languages and voices to a single literature or hegemonic worldview. Such a legacy is coextensive with the life of a poet who enacted in his writings and personal relations a fierce compassion and solidarity with the destitute, the desperate, the disenfranchised.

The strangeness of Saenz's work should be read, in this sense, as the exfoliation of a singular empathy and yearning for otherness. His poems are the flowering of a life given over in fullness to an art that affirms the mysterious unity of all difference, of suffering and ecstasy. Now, as his poetry is translated in Europe and the United States and its appeal and importance are acknowledged, Jaime Saenz, one of Latin America's great poets of the twentieth century, is garnering the international audience his work deserves.

A Note on This Translation

The selections presented in this book span Jaime Saenz's published poetic output between the early 1950s and 1973, the most intense period of his creative activity. In various remarkable styles, Saenz uses rhapsodic language to counter the rhetoric of habit, commerce, and pretension, all of which, Saenz felt, clip the very wings from the word in order to subjugate it, to manipulate it, to keep it from straying beyond the cage of assumed functions and values. With a canny, iterative music, Saenz lures us into folds of syntax that cannot be flattened out into logical assurances or comfortable clarities. That is to say, reading Saenz, we are struck awake to a surging, polyphonic, sometimes tenderhearted, sometimes vexed language of unstable, rapid transitions, a language utterly different from that by which our daily transactions are conducted so often in a semisleep.

Anniversary of a Vision (*Aniversario de una visión*, 1960) is an audaciously emotional love poem in which Saenz accomplishes a syntax equal in complexity to his yearning for the beloved. This syntax, turning in on, mirroring, and extending itself in phrasal strings, enacts a total involvement in the other, and aims, through oxymoron and paradox, to dissolve distinctions between object and subject, lover and beloved, the actor and the acted upon. *Anniversary of a Vision* is a poem both deeply spiritual and linguistically daring, recalling, in that conflation, the great poems of one of Saenz's literary heroes, Cesar Vallejo.

In the poems presented from *As the Comet Passes* (*Al pasar un cometa*, 1970–1972; approximately a third of that book is included here), the reader is introduced to a strange collision of torqued, odd, and romantic images, perhaps an expression of the difficulty, for Saenz, of a loving relationship in a society that didn't countenance homosexuality. We see here not only his mastery of the brief lyric but also, as in "The Basket of Wool" ("La canasta de lana"), his strange and mordant humor, surreal transformations of image, and outlandish juxtapositions in the service of highly energized, even ardent sentiment.

The third section is taken from *The Scalpel* (*El escalpelo*, 1955), Saenz's first published book, one of the most unusual collections in all Latin American poetry, perhaps comparable in its imagistic eccentricities only to the early work of Chilean poet Pablo de Rokha or to that of the Cuban José Lezama Lima. Clearly influenced by Surrealist attitudes and procedures, these prose poems are nevertheless thoroughly nonderivative, bearing an *avant la lettre* attentiveness to energies latent in the material operations of language, something that would remain a signature quality of Saenz's work.

In Bolivia, *To Cross This Distance* (*Recorrer esta distancia*, 1973) is generally considered to be Saenz's master poem, and it is, indeed, an original creation, an existential meditation on presence and absence, love and death, and the imagined possibilities of building a bridge (or reducing the distance) between I and Another. Foregrounded in this poem as well is Saenz's intense contempt for the upper class and for political power. In particular, sections of the poem excoriate, in high pitches of sarcasm and irony, bourgeois culture's losing battle to deny death's leveling reality. But the poem is far from didactic, and its closure is deeply moving in the compassion of its claims.

Finally, *Immanent Visitor* (*Visitante profundo*, 1964), which we have excerpted, is probably the most hermetic and opaque of Saenz's long works. The poem declares itself to "you," to "the other," to a fugitive beloved who might be language itself, a communal and transcendent material beyond the poet's ego. Still, and in keeping with Saenz's manner of punctuating symbolic density with epiphanic clarity, the poem is inlaid with moments of imagistic precision, concluding, brilliantly, with a burst of pure longing in its quartet coda.

Not included in this selection are the serial works *Muerte por el tacto* (Death by feel, 1957) and *El frío*

(The cold, 1967). As well, we do not present here work from Saenz's last three book-length poems, *Bruckner* and *Las tinieblas* (The darknesses; published jointly in 1978), and *La noche* (The night, 1984), Saenz's longest poem. We intend to translate this latter work in the near future.

POEMS IN TRANSLATION

Anniversary of a Vision (1960)

To the image that kindled the lost,
the hidden fires

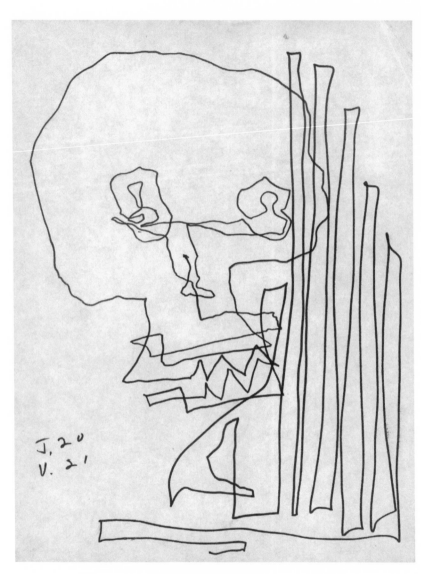

Drawing by Jaime Saenz

I

The floating world is lost, and the whole of life catches in the spring light of your
　　looking,
—and while you repeat yourself in the echo, horizon bound in smoke, I regard
　　your departure,
clear substance and hope dehiscing into distance:
you live on that sweetness when beauty, sorrowing, glances your way,
and you emerge in half-profile
to the iron ringing of nighttime instruments, golden and blue, a music shining and
　　throbbing and taking wing
in the hollow of my heart.

I don't dare look at you lest I not be inside you, and I don't praise you lest joy
　　steal away
—I'm content just to watch you, and you know this and pretend not to look at me
and you bounce around, exaggerating everything with divine insight,
as if you were riding a horse or a motorcycle
—your extravagance amazes me, drills joy into me, it is my daily bread
—when it rains, at a turn of the head, shouts fly from your shoulders,
and you stroke your cheeks and your applause echoes in the water, in the wind,
　　and in the fog
—it amazes me how much I love you!
I yearn for you the moment I hear you,
a sepulchral music vanishes and my death steps out of you,
beloved images become visible to the musicians
when it's you who is listening
—always, the musicians exult in silence
when it's you who is listening.

II

Your crossing the streets separates you from me, as the day and the streets are
    separate
—the whole city is a spider that hoards you from me,
and the light cuts you off; it isolates you and makes me see how well it cocoons
    you
       —resplendent, your happiness on the street corners,
      at grief's hour I ask myself if I will find that sublime, deep blue of your
        garments,
      my nation,
      the air of your voice when evening falls
      —and I ask myself why I would joyously surrender to the joy you kindle in
        me.
Your likeness to me is not to be met in you, in me, nor in my likeness to you
      but in a line randomly traced and made unforgettable by forgetfulness
      —and in the scent rising from certain drawings that make us weep
      and which at the same time enliven us,
      because your stunning vision is a disquiet to the flavor of memories,
      that gentle testimony left by youth of its leaving:
      hidden image,
      taste of youth waiting to blend with the hour of death which is your form
        walking in light and love through the days and the nights and the years
        only to gash my heart
      —my death will have absconded with your gaze, because it reached inside
        you when you searched it out
      though it is wrapped within you and remains there;
      let me name for you its raiment,
      youth will endure in you.

III

You exaggerate without exaggerating because you know that my exaggerations
    make you exaggerate,
and my exaggerations are invisible so that your exaggerations may be visible, not
    only for this age,
and in such subtle manner I add my grain of sand to the discovery of a cure for
    love's malady
—still, I'm alone and bewildered, and need succor in the face of this spasm of
    exaggerations which announce a kind of chaotic glee
—and I don't know if it's you or the devil who bewilders me and makes me see
    what is not seen
and live a life that is neither life nor dream, but fear—a fear of dreaming what my
    soul doesn't know,
a miracle of tenderness and truth transformed into joke when at a butterfly's flight
    I burst into lament
and seeking life and meaning, my struggles and penuries ended up as farce
—because I didn't know we were supposed to impersonate others, being who we
    are,
and we are not what we are, nor do we seem to be what we are,
rather you and I will be, and I will be you also and you will be me,
solely through the grace of imposture
—and, moreover, now I have come to find that love is nothing other than what is
    hidden in love;
and to find it, I will have to transgress what I believe myself to be, which is to say
    you, and come to be you, which is to say me
(in reality, you are because I think, and you are the true reality)
—and you will do the same,
yet don't sigh, don't go here and there,
but where the gaze is firm and sighs are real,

and where a wild bull charges at the mystery
which will unbaptize that it may baptize,
and which will truly name you—from the inside, and not from without.

IV

There being a miracle, there is none; and I call out for the word's effacement, the
    threading of kingdoms and communication through the eyes, the return to the
    soul—you will perish.
        and no one will have seen your soul except me;
        and you, on the other hand, don't even see my face, although I recognize
            yours in the throng,
        when you don't recognize me you believe I believe I'm a flea, and that I
            ignore that I know you and believe I believe as you;
but you should know that were I in fact a flea, even if you looked at me I
    wouldn't know at whom you looked, and I would look at you without feeling
    or understanding the wherefore
—and so, if I am as I was born, it is due to terror, whose son I am; because it
    would not have been out of the question to be born a flea—and of that there's
    no doubt, apparently;
and later, I can wail, as I can wail, and seek the cure to a malady that afflicts not
    me, but you,
someone who, in believing himself to be who he is not, looks at me, as though I
    were what he is, while still being me,
who looks at himself, but not at me, since in truth it is I who believe he looks at
    me,
when he doesn't look at me, because of my looking at him:
so to say, I am I and you are you, and I look at you and for that reason believe

that you look at me, and you don't look at me but believe you do every time you look at me,

except that I don't look at myself but believe I do, looking at you,

which is to say, I am not I and you are not you but I;

in a word: there is and there is not communication; and you don't exist, and I cease to exist in concerning myself with you, since I leave myself so that you may exist

—in conclusion, I'm telling you that this is the tone to use to penetrate matters of love—a dark thing,

for whose explanation the tone will need to be dark, but not lucid;

and I say that common sense only serves to explain itself to itself

for in common sense's tone, you become entombed in your own common sense, believing you've managed to make sense of what you wanted;

dark, very dark the tone must be, if what is hidden in love is to be unleashed;

and the darkness of the tone in the illumination of my farewell from you shall be great indeed,

when I find myself as a body without a body and without you, an aerolite for lack of you,

without the silence of your eyes, without the vision the parting of your lips verged on revealing to me

and without the voyage and the arrival of dream and of light, which enfolded you already to bring you in fullness to me

 —who knows with what gestures, with what somersaults I would have greeted your enchanted apparition!

 —and while I wait years for you and keep myself from living

 and wait for you a minute and live in a rush,

 I would wish for the moon's eclipse just to see my last illusions of kissing you come true,

 it wouldn't matter if half a kiss or no kiss at all and in the flash of darkness or of light

—and my hope, beneath your gaze,
would be the real life I see in the deepness of your eyes.

V

In sight of the river, which cleanses the inhabitants of their morbidity and keeps
them alert,
and which erodes the thin cortex suspending the city, beneath which a great abyss
is hidden,
—I won't address myself to you for a moment, while I long to linger in what you
inhabit and what inhabits you—as it does me,
and make out death's long, anguilliform shape in the strong, wet structure of its
crystal dwelling,
and recognize the way of being and not being of death, which knows how to
grow downward from above
—I want to discover why we feel that we move, in what space, in what place, in
what distance movement moves in stillness,
where movement seeks out a going from one place to the next without needing to
go, and seeks to find itself within immobility and within itself,
like the surface of this river and like its waters, languidly flowing along
with us,
to flow out to the sea, to immerse us and deliver us from not dying
through the absence of death,
which a moment ago was oblivious to our lives,
and which now perches in them, then veers off and away.

The river rushes by thunderous and deaf!—it slides and leaps across the dikes,
at its roar, visions of huge animals incandesce,

the ones we see when, in solitude, we release a strange sadness,
in the transparency and forgetfulness of sighs which the river deepens and
intensifies in the midst of mephitic emanations,
and to the hissing of pure air filtered by Mt. Illimani
which blows over our troubles, our impulsiveness,
those visions battle among sighs and search in the churning waters for a
vision that will envision them and sigh,
and while we breathe the essence of this vast air, filtered, cold, and blue,
at the shadow hour, penetrated to the quick, the mephitic emanations carry us off
to sea,
and dilute us in the roundness of the earth and in an eminence of sky
—I search for you,
and with the dawn and with sighs,
with the clarity of stars the city rises up
—and the river rushes by, disconsolate, and remains.

VI

In the lavish, vaporous light
and in the mountains' ethereal air,
in transparency's solitary immensities and in the columns of smoke, to the fleeting
warmth of the world's somber curving,
—in the streets and in the trees,
the rain reflects the quiet tenderness of your vision.

And out of the graves a sigh sparks the lost and hidden fires
in your charged image,

to the ascension of that melancholic breath, from the darknesses,

    which has ripped open the shrouds of your murmuring ancestors

—and in the bowels of the water, to the measure I hear in oblivion, it rains,

and it rains and I don't look at you; in reality I can see that you look at me,

    —how you look at me!

from some outer reaches of childhood

and from the fathomless seas of youth

    —you look at me in emptiness and across the vast,

how your gaze arrives, from such remoteness and in so moving a way

that it makes me realize I don't look at you!

—and a deep sobbing shakes from me the yearning to meet you,

and talk with you about gratitude, about spring and joy

and about so many other things,

at the same time, I hear you—in the mark on my brow, in a shadow grazing the
wall—

I hear you speaking of everything that makes me cry

—and this is how you answer what I speak in my heart.

VII

May your stay be long beneath the brilliance of the stars

    I leave in your hands my time

    —the rain's time

will perfume your presence, resplendent, in the thicket.

I renounce happiness, I renounce you: you are my soul's body; stay

    —I have gone beyond the twilight and the dross to arrive at the gentle light
of your eyes

and I bury myself in the darkness;
look at no one,
don't open the window. Don't move:
make me know the gesture that, in silence, the breeze broadcasts from your
 mouth:
I am in your memory; make me know if your hands caress me
and if through them the foliage is breathing
—make me know the rain that falls on your secret body,
and whether it is the penumbra that veils it or the night's spirit.

Make me know, lost and vanished vision, what it was your gaze kept cloistered
 from me
  —if it was the desired and secret gift
  that my life waited all its life for death to receive.

From As the Comet Passes

(1970–1972)

Saenz, the middle years

High above the Dark City

One night on a rain-glistened road high above the dark city
with its now-distant tumult
she will certainly sigh
I will sigh
holding hands a long time within the grove
her eyes clear as the comet passes
—her face come from the sea her eyes in the sky my voice inside her voice
her mouth in the shape of an apple her hair in the shape of a dream
in each pupil a look never seen
her eyelashes a trail of light a torrent of fire
everything will be mine somersaulting with gladness
I'll cut off a hand for each of her sighs I'll gouge out an eye for each smile
I'll die once twice three times four times a thousand times
just to expire on her lips
with a saw I'll hack through my ribs to hand her my heart
with a needle I'll draw out my sweetest soul to surprise her
on Friday evenings
with the night air singing a song I propose to live for three hundred years
in the loveliness of her company.

Your Skull

for Silvia Natalia Rivera

These rains,
I don't know why they would make me crave a dream I had, many years back,
containing a dream of yours
—your skull appeared to me

And it had an exalted presence;
it didn't look at me—it looked at you.
And it drew near my skull, and I looked at you.
And when you were looking at me, my skull appeared to you;
it didn't look at you.
It looked at me.

In the exalted night,
someone looked on;
and I dreamed your dream
—beneath a soundless rain,
you hid within your skull,
and I hid within you.

Here

In the distance, in the silence, in the kingdoms of childhood,
someone wept for me.
Your primordial gaze filled all space, and eternity was reborn, and youth.
A drop of water, in place of me.

In the Heights

I looked at you from close up, spring was propitious in the heights.
The splendor visible in all your organs, the revelation of my desire for you,

its source and secret
—and then night fell.

The Basket of Wool

Desiring yet unable, I dreamt myself in this room sleeping and I dreamt myself
    being able,
making a basket of wool toll like a bell to keep myself sleeping,
and wanting them to come not come, and to make not make a basket of wool toll
    like a bell prompting a sadness without desire,
eliciting a Japanese music that makes me weep remembering but not hearing,
summoning an unsummonable scene that pure luck renders summonable,
as when one says:
now that this lady summons speaking and that gentleman speaks summoning,
as when one says:
"Come here, little parrot; let's make this basket of wool toll like a bell," leaving
    everyone happy with this Japanese music that makes me weep, in summoning,
and which goes on eliciting and tolling and goes on playing through the night.

So I Am Persuaded

for Jaime Taborga V.

Everyone lives in one
—I, you, they.
We all live in all, no one lives or dies, and each is on his own
—but nobody knows what happens.

The world is a conjecture, so I am persuaded.

The form you attribute to yourself, the one I attribute to myself, the world
assumes.

Movement and form are one and the same, and there is no such thing as the
roundness of the world,

but indeed there is a form that ceaselessly transforms itself by virtue of time's
movements

condensing and expanding into spirals already, into essences and lives, or into the
kingdoms of chaos,

to return to the primordial particle, or to trail off into far regions of the decreated
and the uncreated,

where nothing happens no matter what might happen, and where everything
happens no matter what may not;

which is precisely where form's first and final cause must be found,

so I am persuaded.

The City

for Blanca Wiethüchter and Ramiro Molina

With the smoke and with the fire, many people muffled and silent
on a street, on a corner,
in the high city, pondering the future in search of the past
—in the subtle entrails, night lightning,
in the probing eye, thoughts go to agony.

In another age, hope and happiness were good for something—time's flow
invisible,

and the darkness, an invisible thing,

was revealed but to the infinite elders fumbling forward to feel if you might not
be among them,

while fumbling to touch some children they think they feel, even though these
little ones feel them and are confused with them, feeling you,

as in solitude you feel a shawl of darkness woven with unfathomed sadness by
some habitant,

dead and lost in this transparent darkness that is the city I myself inhabit,

inhabiting a city at the base of my soul which is inhabited but by a single habitant,

—and like a city filled with sparks, filled with stars, filled with fires on street
corners,

filled with coals and embers in the wind,

like a city where many beings, alone and distant from me, move and murmur with
a destiny heaven no longer knows.

with eyes, with idols, and with children smashed by that very heaven

with no more life than this life, with no more time than this time,

hemmed-in by the great wall of fire and oblivion, rocking in the swing of despair,

soundlessly weeping with this sinking city.

And no angel or demon in this well of silence.

Only fires lining the long streets.

Only the cold contours of shadows, the indifference of the sun pulling back.

The breath of a dawn for the last time breaking, the doors creaking in wind,

the boundaries breaking up and scattering and forms fusing with the flames,

the signs and the songs,

with a remote anguish, in soil and beyond soil,

and the breathing of the dead, the incessant rains,

resignation with its taste of bread, in a house that stalks me between dreams,

the patios and the steps, the beings and the stones, and hallways without end,

the windows opening to emptiness and shutting to shock,
the rooms where I lose myself and the corners where I hide
—the dark walls and the wet moss, the outposts where I look for I don't know
  what,
hiding myself from the rising stench of habit.

No voice, no light, no testimony of my former life.
Only the fires,
undying though forever flickering, and only the fires.
The desolate portent of the ghost once named youth
—in my city, in my dwelling.

Watching the River Flow

for Leonardo García-Pabón

When the hour comes I'll speak with you, watching the river flow, at the river's
  edge.
With the profile of your face, with the echo of your voice, parceling out my voice
  into the depths,
into the great spaces that death's eye has seen, you will know the hidden word.
Where the wind stills. Where living is finished off and all color is one.
Where water is not touched and where earth is not touched: inside my invisible
  presence, where you know yourself to be, in the millenary present
—of deeds, of smells and of forms; of animals, of minerals, of plants inside time.
In time, of time. Inside premonition's root. Inside the seed, inside anguish,
only you will know the hidden word.

The aloneness of the world. The aloneness of man. Man's reason for being and
   the world's
—the circular solitude of the sphere. Increment and decline;
the closing of the hermetic thing. The hermetic closing of the thing.
The immense, the immeasurable—the incommensurate grave, indivisible and
   blank.

Someone Must Be Called Twilight

for Carlos Ramírez

Through the years the glow persists.
The horizon, where my steps echo and go out with the twilight, persists.
The rains of spring, the waiting that begins when the year closes up, and the
   ceaselessly appearing vision;
this sky of spirits, this sky of things and shadows; the fall of evening persists.
The dead, the stones and songs persist; the clouds and the din and the lives;
the darkness, the world and the distance.
Through the tunnel of years, the glow persists.
Because nothing can swallow itself but real life which lives on the glow that
   swallows it.

Many times searching without being able to find you, the twilight would
   surprise me in the hour of your eyes.
Many times I forgot you, wanted to forget myself and remember, and
   remembered I had to forget you,
thinking of you for the very reason I didn't want to remember you

—the twilight would surround me at such times, I remember it perfectly.
I confused you with the twilight confusing myself with you;
you confused me with the twilight confusing yourself with me,
and you and I confused ourselves with the twilight which confused you in me and
me in you,
confusing with you what was confused in me to confuse with me what was
confused in you.
And many times in the same person there was a confusion of twilight, you and
me,
and many more each confused with three other distinct persons,
adding up to nine altogether, which is to say, zero.

And there was no such person called twilight,
or, to tell the truth, no person not called twilight,
except those called you and I, who nevertheless could not keep from calling each
other twilight.

From The Scalpel (1955)

Saenz in beggar's coat

Homage to Epilepsy

THESE ARE THE LITTLE EPILEPTIC'S HAIRS

The little epileptic's hairs grow out darkly at the break of night. Their resins flow into undulant ends, and they seem like colossal columns of granite in the glorious and mysterious field of love and death.

Within these hairs, which I respect as beings unto themselves, there are swings of baffling roundness on which I see the black magic and love of space.

These are the hairs of the dead one in the span of a hand that has fingered the mystery.

THE COACH OF THE DEAD

A long time ago, when I was a child, they tried to teach me things about certain things. But I never managed to grasp the norms of discipline.

One day I was walking through the city and I saw a coach. It caused me great distress. I don't know, now, if it was green or blue or red, but over the course of my life I came to believe it was colorless, that it was simply a coach.

On that day when, as a child, I saw the coach, I was infected with who knows what strange force, what strange presentiments.

It was the coach of the dead, according to the revelation of the epileptic child I encountered years later on a sunny afternoon . . .

This incident, of course, means little at all, given that the child refers to any passing coach as the "coach of the dead."

The dead, just like the living, can die again.

So the revelation of the epileptic child, on a sunny afternoon.

The dead have the power to die.

The fact of dying deprives no one of the right to die again. Here lies the secret to existence.

This is why the dead have died.

This is also why the dead are, in a sense, precocious.

THE DOOR THAT OPENS TO MYSTERY

It's possible to conjure a door, not a door through which children pass into a timeless room, but an authentic door that opens into mystery.

To conjure a preamble to lunacy, so that all those who fabricate nothing have no idea what to do.

That child, I know, harbors secrets to a door that might lead into mystery while bypassing, let me be clear, the attendant putrefactions.

There is a door. That door is open to you, to me, to everyone. It is open to the rats considering you night after night from the moon.

The child must be allowed to go on with some of his hairs and a piece of the door to mystery before he stops recognizing the streets and rocks.

(This is the secret of the door.)

A SNUFFED MATCH

A snuffed match is simply a snuffed match. The transcendence of a snuffed match lies in its being snuffed and in the fact that although it no longer exists, it is still called a match.

But that match there, on a sheet of paper, is dead. That is what matters. What really matters is that it be dead.

It is being, itself, and being there, it must be acknowledged to be as large as the universe. Like something that folds itself into the intervals of nothingness.

SHROUD THAT SHIELDS SILHOUETTE PAPERS

It's a shroud. I'm sure everyone has seen a shroud in childhood, if only in stories. Everyone in childhood has seen shrouds and shrouds. Nevertheless, I have begun to put the shrouds of the whole world into a deep freeze.

Suddenly I am back in my room. I see a freshly washed shroud, but it's only a joke.

I sleep in worn, moonspotted sheets and dream of shrouds.

They cover me, they soundlessly fasten me to my coming putrefaction, the torches grind themselves out over my glorious body in the middle of the night. Later, inside magic, they come to life, wrapping me up with the creatures of fate.

They are papers cut out by the moon. It's necessary to let them lie there, where the hapless tables are sleeping, all of them, all of them, the hapless spiders, it's necessary to let them lie just as they are, in the music of their child-shrouds.

The silhouette papers blow across the world carrying the melancholy stigmata of good-byes.

THE FATHOMLESS HOWL

It's merely a fathomless howl. It comes from far off. It has nothing to do with the womb, with the lungs, or the liver. It is, simply, a howl after which you want to leave serenely for the moon, taking along a few hairs from a certain gifted child. "A fathomless howl," I have been told, "is the howl of all humankind, always."

IMAGE OF THE CHILD

So sweet is his image. No one can see it, save the snail rooted to seashore.

No one can see it, except the spiders that live where you live, where the haunting organic gears of eternity live.

Nothing can hold back his childhood-desire.

This is how his image is. The life of the illusory images of death and life.

He has a design.

The design is an outline of love and death's secret, though the child is blind to love and death, though with his homage to epilepsy, it swells into a vague omnipotence.

(Pure and lifeless object for harvesting loneliness.)

THE CATASTROPHE AND THE PHASES OF THE EYE WITH DEATH

Everything ends now. Sublime catastrophe.

Here in the night's heart, I have paid homage to the mysterious epileptic, just so, and with the meekness of a lake.

I offer my homage. Soundlessly, catastrophe comes. The needles point to the sky. It will always be this way.

The eyes turn yellow and make a lattice over the other things that are not. The life that is real is about to arrive.

Paraphrase of "So Have You Told Him or Not?"

The paraphrase of what she had said is a reflection of Wiesbaden. Rainy and fleeting as she is, luminous as she is, and with that quick gift she has for disappearing into the throng, having passed within five centimeters of me, without even knowing me, or as if we had met on the shore of some immense ocean with wooly floor, with fish blazing across its surface, their backs puffed out, their spines rigid and splayed. Fish with a marvelous gift for the particular. They call you by name, though you scarcely believe it. Unlike other genera of fish, these are able to roll their eyes to follow your movements, and they are able (this is a remarkable case of devotion) to abandon the sea and drag themselves over sand until they expire, and for no other reason than to discharge their one duty, which is to follow you through the rabid and aimless multitude.

But, needless to say, you are not the multitude. Rather, you are its essence, the very being of multitude. It is understood, the multitude radiates outward from you, and it is understood down to the bones of grief that there would be no multitude were it not of your making. This is why I love not only the multitude, but multitudes. I love it and I love them because I have a concept of you that is big with eternity, and because the primordial weather for learning some slender stretch of anguish consists of the multitude and the multitudes, into which, into it and into them, you have breathed life by that miraculous enigma of the word spoken and heard across a few centimeters: "So have you told him or not?"

What it is I am making, and what I call "Paraphrase of 'So have you told him, or not?'" is nothing more than an incidence of distant, vague conjectures, of black, fierce, and lucid imaginings about you, when once I (I, I myself) had my arms outstretched to the wind, the scent, let's say, of Wiesbaden—like this evening—and a translucent skull.

The Candle and the Breeze (Excerpt)

One man is thrust into fire, while another notes his misfortune from the water's edge without taking into account the idea of the flame with which the candle struggles, flickering and far from those realities in which the world is transfigured into platter or kidney, or in which a tomato might exude the feeling of a fine, rose hue in equipoise to the burning throats of children, be they beautiful or pox ridden or tightrope walkers.

By chance, have you ever seen the nucleus of the flame, and have you not been startled by the marvel of it? Have you ever thought about the fires of the hands, the fires of the neck, the fires of the convent at dawn while you search for something like a holy stone to swallow; have you ever thought of the child's scarlet fever, thought of him clotted with forests, immersed in melancholy, allegoric and brittle, wracked by the wild storm, slick from soap, intrinsically doughy, with his elongated neck and his monstrous lips, his shirt in tatters, with the aroma of flowers around his shoulders and knees?

There is, in his demeanor, a preternatural candle that measures out destiny. There is, above all, in his clothes, a tiny gauge by which the fire and breeze are metered.

If you see something blazing, you remember the flame. If you see the sea, you remember it; and if you see clods of dirt on the wide and dry roads, you remember it.

There is an interval of pebbles and party-noise when you light a candle to bestow a certain allegory upon his death, so tiny, so sad, rainy and circled by fire.

E.

"E"; you know what "E" means.

"E" means the first death, the root one, one's own death, which leaves the others waiting horribly alone and smug to be alive, scrubbed with the best soaps.

That's what "E" means. "E," so dead and quiet and architectonic as you, experimenting with whether or not to use it, saying "I'm here," "one," "were," "fear," "hope," "petticoat," "Caquiaviri," "then," "Erasmus"; or better, "student," "we're on our way to my father's house," "I am here to invite you all to crumpets," "illusion," "don't tickle gentlemen on the bus," "it seems like they insist on not putting the leashes where they belong," "grooves," "the faggots have not yet been taken from the oven," "a couple brothers want to sell their coffee shop, but for cash," "the clothes are wet," "you always want to have it your way," "sewer drain."

That's how "E" is.

Deafening and curious, like rain; you can't suit "E" or "T" to any other letter of the alphabetum, to the candle or the breeze.

The candle and the breeze are beings apart. Each unknowing the other. Your sadness spokes outward from this unknowing. It is the interregnum between your soul and the candle and the breeze.

Now go and sleep with the dark things you are always seeking and never finding.

The Voyage of the Lindens and the Madrepores while Rocking in the Weariness of the Age-Old Cradles (Excerpt)

They walk in the echo. They walk darkly, as trances walk. They walk disrupting the rhythms, they walk with that anguished night-whistling, lugging their howling, sublime emissaries. They walk on their buttocks, the pubis forgotten. But more than anything, they walk so assertively it is frightening.

You are not to forget it. They walk straining their being, they walk as if another walked in them, they walk on, terrifying, full of themselves, puffed up, fervent.

They walk like no one walks. They keep walking, even lying down at someone's side. They walk awake and asleep, they walk backward, they walk out of step, visited by rare dispensations.

They walk as if someone had commanded: "Don't walk."

(With the magnet on their backs, they know and don't know where they walk. But they are led to the vexed, formidable core of smiles forgotten in the coursing river, in the echo rising—I don't know how—from the piano and the cello, in the zenith of a cold and bewildering evening. Night, inescapably, had to fall.)

—■—

They are the inventors of noise, you know this. They bid farewell with a noise, with a cunning, bitter noise.

They take their crumbs noisily to the sea, and they get up, they lie down, and they materialize noisily, with the ironic, pleasing, prophetic noise of good-byes. They are formidable.

They are the enigmatic form of weeping. Without knowing it, they have plotted out the clever schemes, the oblique, universal, eternal schemes.

The intuited manners of felt rhythm, of the tender ruckus to which one wakes. The intuited magical manners of premonition, the exalted manners of the square and the circle; the odd, invisible manners, those with double gestures, those of spent ecstasy, of spent woe, of inmost supplication, those of the astonishing grief-crossing.

They are the first finders of melancholy. They are, in their hushed terror, pre-cursors to the voyage's figure. The voyage's mode of displacing no one, not even the travelers.

They are figures both vague and precise, bestial angels, supreme, assumed, real, catastrophic, ideal symbols. They are decent and full of quiet, and they are, on this night, fantastic universes, huge beckonings of nothingness, cries spurted from bone, memorial instigators of your smile.

To Cross This Distance (1973)

To the image of Puraduralubia

Saenz taking a break

I

I am divided from myself by the distance I find myself in,
the one who is dead is divided from death by a great distance.
I plan to cross this distance, resting along the way.
Face up, in the dwelling of desire,
stock still, in my place—opposite the locked door,
with a winter's light at my side.

In the corners of my room, in the chair's arena.
With wavering memory splitting off from the void
—on the ceiling of the vault,
the one who is dead must communicate with death.

Contemplating the bones on the plank, numbering the darknesses with my fingers
    starting from you.
Seeing that things are, I fill with desire.
And I find myself crossing a great distance.

II

Like nocturnal air, the Festival of the Spirit is a finished thing,
like the ladder—leaning against a wall to hear the word—is a finished thing,
like the line I once traced, the line your shadow fled, is a finished thing.

Like the smoke in the braziers with the incense and the vapors spreading,
longing for voices,
like the lights and the mirrors rising toward the winter skies,

with the vanished memory of the customs and of those who are definitively
  distant in the distance,
thus it is that the implements and the skulls are no longer implements nor skulls,
in the ceremonies of winter, they are no longer used.

III

At the touch of the fleeting secret, of stopped time, of self-consuming fire, and of
  ice, present and eternal,
every eye, every image, will blaze up and burn.
Every hollow within the earth, every darkness that falls, will forever remain.
(If you're a sorcerer, laugh. But if not, hearing that the devil is on your tail, don't
  laugh.)
With the passing of the years and the turning of these worlds and the lights I've
  gathered from contemplating the stars, I've become aware.
In the torrential waters every soul dissolves into universal soul.

IV

The immense malaise cast by shadows, the melancholic visions surging from the
  night,

everything terrifying, everything cruel, that without reason, that without name,
one has to take it, who knows why.

If you have nothing to eat but garbage, don't say a word.
If the garbage makes you sick, don't say a word.
If they cut off your feet, if they boil your hands, if your tongue rots, if your spine
    splits in two, if your soul fines down to nothing, don't say a word.
If they poison you, don't say a word, even if your bowels slide from your mouth
    and your hair stands straight up; even if your eyes well with blood, don't say a
    word.
If you feel good, don't feel good. If you fall behind, don't fall behind. If you die,
    don't die. If you're sad, don't be sad. Don't say a word.
Living is hard; it's hard work not to say a word.
Putting up with people without saying a word is tough.
It's very hard—inasmuch as they expect to be understood without saying a
    word—
to understand people without saying a word.
It's terribly difficult yet very easy to be a decent person;
the truly difficult thing is not to say a word.

V

The hatred which the father who is son professes to the son who is father is father
    of the hatred which the son who is father professes to the father who is son.
Everyone conspires against everyone and each bites and tears apart the other;
    they never starve and they eat shit, whether they actually eat shit or don't eat
    it, traffic or don't traffic in silks and liquors and all kinds of commodities,

they laugh at humankind and cut diamonds, they stop and take up dominoes, now
  racing, now betting on everything,
they go to the country and sail at their leisure, they travel by train, they fly by
  plane, they eat cookies and pass out kisses and greetings,
well-pleased with their spit-shined shoes, with their slick, styled hair, with their
  bronzed complexions, and their crocodile-skin wallets.
They grow thoughtful reading the papers, they sigh with calculated restraint, they
  cough with self-satisfaction and fall ill every now and then, as prescribed by
  rituals of decorum,
and you just have to see the look they get as they climb into the jet.
The majestic air they adopt when they're talking shop, their severity when they
  mention ethics,
the casual grace with which their noses are blown, that slight tilt of the head, that
  pleasantness, that I don't know what with which they grin,
you just have to see that rare people-person way, the zeal, the assertiveness, the
  knack, the secret charm they exude in all their exploits,
and the animus in the gesture; that disconcerting subtlety with which they hold
  forth on art and psychology,
the wise judgment and authority on human pain, and with what anguish they offer
  their opinion;
you just have to see the enormous nobility of the look with which they forgive
  the failings of mere mortals;
the consummate technique with which they chew and swallow a thousand pills to
  keep themselves plump and rosy;
the stylishness with which they arrive to consult the shrink, just in time to check
  their watch and get nervous—
a little nervous, not too much, with aristocratic smirk and nobleness of visage;
you just have to see the stunning grace with which they move in the world and
  the importance they concede to their lives;

the transcendent meaning in every motion and, even more, in each of their
   nervous tics, even when they have none;
you just have to see the heroic poses, the facility with which they assume a fierce
   tone of voice,
the tremendous audacity of resolve as they die of fright, the shudder in the asshole
   when they freeze with fear,
and the *ayees* and the *yikes*, the *owies* and the *yowies*, when they cry for help the
   moment they sense their precious lives besieged by some ghost,
and the cock-strut they do to hide the terror that consumes them;
you just have to see what awaits them, a demon coiling inside,
which will rend them apart without pause or pity, thanks to your silence and by
   deed of your silence.

VI

I feel the coming of a dark day, a closed space, an incomprehensible event, a night
   endless as immortality.
What I feel has nothing to do with me, nor with you; it's nothing personal,
   nothing particular, this thing I feel;
but it has to do with I don't know what
—perhaps the world, or kingdoms of the world, or the mysterious enchantments
   of the world;
one looks and sees, across the waters, a profound fissure.
One can perceive, through the odor of things and through the forms they assume,
   the exhaustion of things.
In what grows, in what has ceased to grow, in what echoes, in what stays, in what
   doesn't stay, in the soundless air, in the metamorphosis of the insect, in the
   murmuring of trees,

one can sense the joy of a coming end.

The devouring darknesses, dying to devour—the finale finished. Nothing more
 to be.

Save perhaps a mist, high above some place, maybe deep inside some place,
wafting across the farthest waters.

The gasping without end or beginning, a shroud for stillness,
enshrouding the circular motions of the eternal return
 —I don't know how to explain, I don't know how to name this feeling I feel.

VII

At the inexplicable site, exactly where ruin and reunion have taken place,
the loveliness of life is a truth that one neither can nor should deny.

> The beauty of life,
>
> through the miracle of living.
>
> The loveliness of life,
>
> which remains,
>
> through the miracle of dying.

Life flows, passes and soars, coils into an unreachable innerness.
In the aura of the passersby, at the very quick,
in the wind, quavering with the leaving and coming of the passersby,
in the sayings, in the pleadings, in the shouts, in the smoke
 —in the streets, with a light sometimes on the walls, and other times with a
 darkness.
In that gazing upon things with which animals tend to gaze;

in that gazing of the human, with which the human tends to gaze at the gaze of
the animal gazing upon things.
In the weave of cloth,
in iron where iron is iron.
In the table,
in the house.
In the river's edge.
In the moisture of the air.
In the heat of summer, in the cold of winter, in the light of spring
—in an opening and closing of eyes.
Tearing open the horizon or entombing itself in the abyss,
real life rears its head and goes under.

VIII

In a burning and pulsing force I long for enchantment.
In the ancient silence of a wind I long for enchantment.
In the isolate world from which nothing flows, save only lost enchantment, which
returns me to you,
I long for the gallows where once I saw myself hanging to gaze fully at you,
in all your movements, your ways
—I long for the years, the dates, the exact days that are called today,
the exact instants that are called now—the tomorrow that has been, the yesterday
that is to be,
I long for a certain wound that was yours, that gathered into a certain wound that
was mine,
which tunneled into the abyss of your eyes
—into the abyss of your eyes, in which I long for the abyss of your eyes.

IX

With shadows and prodigious pirouettes the jugglers emerge from the night.
With elbows and kicks they force their way through the crowd of stunned
  celebrities who stare dazzled.
Suddenly, they roll out to the center of the ring, doing stunts.
They cinch their belts and tumble into the jumble of dwarf ponies who just now
  appear; they wink their eyes and keep tumbling,
and they sip coffee and eat apples, they do this, do the other thing, and do
  something else altogether,
and this is what they do, and the other thing, and something else altogether, and
  not something else, until the stage resounds as someone comes on,
and eating garlic the whistle-blower makes the rafters resound
and everyone cowers and hunches over, and withdraws inward, and is absorbed in
  thought,
in the midst of a deep silence that reigns the lights go up, the lights don't go up,
  the lights go off,
to the spell of bewitched dogs bursting into the ring doing spectacular flips,
uncertainty descends and then doesn't descend with the bewitched dogs
who begin to trot all around the roundness of the circle in finest style,
  surmounting obstacles that are inherently insurmountable,
with graceful contortions and with suitable and regal step,
very conscious of the admiring admiration with which the admired admirers
  admire them,
with thousands and thousands of eyes that anxiously turn and roll with the spins
  and spinnings of an apparatus that is truly ostentatious,
of perilous trajectories, truly intricate, but not nonsensical.
And with the dust they kick up, and with the sawdust they kick up, and with the
  ponies they kick up, and with the jugglers they kick up, and with the garbage
  they kick up, and with the midgets these bewitched dogs kick up,

a lady of a beauty never seen rises up, and, after removing her eyeballs and
wiping her spectacles, after letting rip a scream, she passes out,

and gibberish abounds, exaltation abounds, chocolate and joy, in joyous hearts, to
the rhythm of the general delight,

to the rhyme with which these bewitched dogs rise up, for the reason of removing
one's eyes, in the rhyme of wiping one's spectacles, for the reason of letting rip
a scream and passing out, without rhyme or reason, to the rhythm of universal
consternation,

to the rhyme of a hound blown all out of proportion, for the reason of throwing
itself into barking, in the rhyme of leaping, for the reason of wetting the wall,
in the rhyme of clawing up the post that supports the hounds, for the reason of
going off with them,

to the rhyme of interring themselves in an indeterminate and unknown world,
hostile, thick with burrs and devoid of daisies,

to the rhythm of an earthly man washing his hands, so generous, so giving, so
kind,

who looks at them with impotent rage and snorts like a bellows,

with pathetic gestures of astonishment, with powerful magnetic stares,

with the neck of a bull and a devil's horns, with the head of a plover and the back
of an ursus, with a blowfly buzzing in the skull,

with powdered cheeks and gloved hands, advancing with hasty and desperate step,

who enters and sits center ring, making sorrowful signs and then starts to weep,

provoking a circular movement at the expense of the crowd which, in effect, spills
forth in a scramble to surround the stricken one,

engendering a ring with a hundred little ringlets thanks to many other people who
have emerged from nothing less than nothingness,

thanks to the sorrowful signs made by the stricken one hoping to avoid just that,

except that all the disguises and masks and foremen, the incompetent and the
competent surround him, all the motley and makeup and the characters, with
the tributes and rituals of flatter,

the mortals and immortals, large and small, white and black, women and not-women, men and not-men surround him,

implicated and not implicated in the signs he makes, while he makes those he doesn't make but doesn't make them, which he doesn't unmake but makes, except what he makes; and this is what he makes.

X

In the world's deep realms are great spaces
—a nothingness ruled over by nothingness itself,
which is cause and origin of the first terror, of thought and echo.
Inconceivable depths exist, hollows before whose allure, before whose haunting spell,
one would surely and simply die.
Sounds one would surely yearn to hear, forms and visions one would surely yearn to see,
things one would surely yearn to touch, revelations one would surely yearn to know,
who knows with what secret yearning and coming to know who knows what.

In the essential soul of the world's synchrony and duration,
buried in the abyss from which the world arose, and embedded in the marrow of the world,
an odor can be sensed, which you will recognize at once, for you have never known another like it;

the odor of truth, the only one, the odor of the abyss—and you will have to
know it.
Because only when you come to know it will you understand how it's always been
true that wisdom coheres in the absence of air.

In the deepest darkness of the world, wisdom will offer itself, in the hermetic
kingdoms of the soul;
in the vicinities of fire and in fire itself, in which the selfsame fire together with air
is devoured by the darkness.
And it is because no one has any idea of the abyss, and because no one has known
the abyss, nor has sensed the odor of the abyss,
that wisdom cannot be spoken of among men, among the living.
While alive, man will not be able to understand the world; man ignores the fact
that as long as he doesn't leave off living, he will not be wise.
He fears everything that borders on wisdom; as soon as he can't understand, he
distrusts
—he understands nothing outside the living.

And I say that one should strive to be dead.
To do so at all costs, before dying. One would need to do everything possible to
be dead.
The waters tell you of it—fire, air, and the light, in clearest speech.
To be dead.
Love tells you of it, the world and all manner of things, to be dead.
Darkness tells nothing. It is pure silence.

One has to think of the sealed spaces. Of the vaults opening beneath the oceans.
Of the caverns and the grottoes—one has to think of the fissures, of the infinite
    tunnels in the umbrae.
If you think of yourself, all your soul and body, you will be the world—in its
    innerness and in its visible forms.
Become accustomed to thinking intently of one thing; everything is dark.
What is true, what is real, what exists; being and essence, it is one and dark.
Thus, darkness is the world's law; fire fans the darkness and goes out—it is
    devoured by darkness.
I say this: it is necessary to think of the world—what is inside the world gives me
    much to think about. I am dark.
I'm not interested in thinking of the world beyond the world; light is interrupting,
    as is living—which is transitory.

What could living ever have to do with life; living is one thing, life is another.
Life and death are one.

XI

A distance crossed, an uninhabited city. In a lost city,
an inhabited city—time never was.
The rain's reflection, another rain.
A greeting, a sign—they greet you and they go.
A melody heard, a forgetting—a forgetting and who knows what,
        a spell of emptiness,
        a scent,
        a glance

—which memory does not drain off, which memory does not wash back.
And that is all.
Nothing and no one remains; it is one.
It all remains with one, and nothing remains
—matter, the earth. What is not touched, what is touched,
what is not,
everything is and remains.
What has been, what is, what is to be, there is no time
—there is nothing—everything is.

Don't feel hurt
—don't hurt one bit.
Time never was; nothing has ever been; the human has everything
—hope is a grave thing.
To say farewell and become the farewell,
that is fitting.

XII

What hand will have been touched by this hand.
What mouth will have been kissed by this mouth.
What eyes will have been seen by these eyes.
Amid what paths, amid what darknesses, will these eyes have gazed at me.
Where will this hand have been found by my hand; when will this hand have
been revealed by my hand.
On what day, what hour, in what place, will I have found this body and this soul I
love.

In what mysterious moment will I have found my soul and my body to love as I
do this soul and this body that I love.

—■—

This body, this soul, are here.
I am and here am I in this soul, in this body, in this soul that I love and this body
that I love.
By way of its breath, in the invisible and the concealed, I found this soul.
In the way of gazing out and being of this body—in the way of being of its
vestment,
in the vestment's dark and subtle way of being present and not present, I found
the secret,
I found presence.

With a sound echoing here, with a remote antiquity,
in this distance
rain is falling;
with a gentle breeze of shadows and lights, in which this phantasmal country
vanishes bit by bit
—with a throbbing and with a song,
with a dream that is far down, this being sleeps in the splendors of a limbo,
in the flickering splendors of a limbo.

From very distant places, from very deep spaces,
with the breath of joy in which the earth is swaying,
an air arrives
—the air that arrives at the latest hour, charged with premonition.

At enchantment's final hour, in which the earth sinks away somewhere,
 beyond the wall,
 where this body that I love is lying,
 where this soul that I love is lying.

 Beyond the beyond of all the paths,
 in the transcendence of the scent of this body that I love,
 in the transcendence of the scent of this soul that I love.

From Immanent Visitor (1964)

*Your serious happiness flows out behind you in an
ecstasy of ancient voyage.*

*For my mother and my Aunt Esther;
and for my dead friends.*

Saenz at his desk in his study

I

This immanent visitor haunts lilies and the body's delicate down, he adorns a
    penumbra.
He roams the chords and the manifold contours, and here, in the window and
    there, in the magnificent forest,
this wayfarer gazes at me, unreadable,
veils himself in the dense and pungent smell of lamps
and in those intricate weavings oblivion loomed
—the felicitous slips into the periphery
of his marble stare, washed and smooth,
his gaze and grace and flourished baton orchestrate a song for the fossiled stars
and from below and above undulate the flux and curve of an undergrowth of
    dreams
which our steps flatten without pity to the ground.
A flame hovers over the prattle, ensombers the wine's sediment,
and proclaims the arrival of a corpse to the rituals of morning
—light-fearing, the dead one, with ears of gold and cacao,
a torso engraved in his memory,
tears lovely as spiders
and hands alert in their place,
amid the stillness of the psalms.

III

From the blue way you envelop the world,
the blue way you adore it.
I'm saddened and in love with your blue way—with the blue way of presence in
    which you attend my readiness to live and die in this world.

With the blue way in which the idea conducts you to gesture's inception—you
    sense the great roaring you live, and you interpret and explain it for your kind
    and for us
at the water's edge, the ear tuned to the revelations of a lily transmuting light's
    desire on a plain of shifting sands, and the measured turns of the wheel
    foretelling the idea-child and the event's first and final virtue.
With the blue way in which you gather your thought
    —the blue way you cast on that lunar trace, when man surrendered his smile to
    the stars.

From the time before my beginning, I only keep from you the terror of being
    born and of giving birth, and the terror of being dead, that others die or are
    dead,
because—odd case of forgetfulness—I no longer know your remote teaching.
I no longer know what you instilled in me, nor will I know it, even dead;
it's an odd case of forgetfulness, blue way,
and we'll shake and wobble until your kind and us and our kind and you pass into
    thou
the one likeness there, waiting to uncode your living and dying.

When you allow us and this beautiful world to wound you,
and you pretend to stumble, or sleep, and feign to have been seen or hint that
    someone has spied a trace of you,
and with a bolt of light you radiate fear and surprise into our world,
we will come round to gaze out from the animal, from the dead and from the
    living and from the guts of our world,
and we'll never again forget. It will be redemption, blue way.

The musician and the rifles, lightness, heaviness and the shade, the nicknames, the
  cotton and the cramp, hatred, the swindlers, the magpie, age and the padlocks,
  spelling and the café and the liars, the flea and ivory, the number, the bees, the
  vision and me, the tail, the gold and the shelves and the frail,
we await the sign, eager to fuse into each other and continue the dialogue with
  you, blue way.

May the days stretch on and the nights be hazy and the blowflies blessed with
  bearable life.
May this be so and so much more
—may man cease to follow the animals and arrive at the human, the sublime, and
  the true
—may wool not be stolen from the animal and each and every being be left in
  peace.

Now a scream is heard, screamed who knows why.
It's not a human scream nor an animal's, but the scream of a thing
—its origin is here, and it seems unthinkable
—blue way, I am saddened and bewildered forever.
It is my intention to cease to see myself and to leave off knowing myself, and I
  will eat myself, should you not be able to make yourself seen.

V

Because the day nourishes dry dreams and wounds your angelical being,
you will set off in search of night

—and I'll tell you that she likes to ask, like a mendicant, for the whole of life: she
hardly ever takes pity.
But you, with your incredibly tender way,
are communicative, and you will move her in that vaulted light if you say:
"I want death but not the dying"
—and those at rest beyond the fire will hear the startled word of your flight and
seeing how they would have adored you, they won't want to know they are
dead.
And in this way you'll know the chimeras of the night
and what is unspeakable of death in your shape,
my joy: I am standing and with a fire in my hands.

(At night, your white-fringed clothes reflect a music of cities and suns and allow
another, denser vestment to be seen, which makes the bridges quiver and the
voyages embark, and seats the night in your eyes.)

VI

Under darkness, pain drives the ancient force with which you arouse the verdure's
fragrance
—in the splendors the heart will lift from mountains, in the forgetfulness of great
bells,
in the dilated and hardened poles of the hymns is the pivotal chord that shocks
you into seeing:
one pole of the magnet goes blank, and you adjust the cadence of your fingers to
the smoke's leisurely climb.

Under aloneness, at the hour of bewilderment and amazement, evening falls;
toward great depths and displacements, the horizon bears your weight,
and the dead one is ardent, worldly in the sea froth, in murmurings and in light
—and the water begins to boil, prophecy makes the rounds.

It shines in grottoes and on your lips, and the current in your dreams won't
    slacken,
a bell's clapper separates you from night's camisole;
I won't perish until you lay an egg in everlasting testimony to that current.

VII

Alive at the edge of language, the head floating in a body not there
a finger in the fog
the running water in the world of those who embroider their presence with a
    border of flax
and another finger in wind that swings the suns of a miracle named by summer
    and rain
and the ancientness of light still unrobed, unseen
then one night another finger twitching to a vague melody on the bridge
and the heaviness of sobbing in the bouquet, bequeathed from offspring to
    offspring
when the swollen fury of the gleaming torrent roars past
but the bond calls you and calls you and another finger, sheathed in flame, prods
    and prods your heart
—you bat your eyes at the magical sign that orbits your body and licks at
    stubborn life

—you're on the way to a city, and someone straining and straining to be born
   snaps the lighter off
and you eat his desire and the cauldron of a drum disenchants itself before your
   eyes.
Fibers and sounds, scattered on the ground, find something of their first secret in
   you
and the measured throb of nocturnal murmurs arrives triumphant
one could say that the mill swelled and the lives were resurrected before the
   clouds,
shed your husk, admit the genuine, and you will fly over the watery deep
—each May, each instant, and each year it is possible to say whether the true
   water is occluded,
whether the fire is hidden and burns you
—and so
shed your husk quickly, because everything is shedding itself.

There are hidden cities hiding cities in their hearts, and the first day their
   brilliance reigns, and the last day is a lost memory shining in man's eye
—their streets make explicit the world and suggest its summit, and the spiral is
   fragrant with hair and skulls
—from you to me, from them to them, from all to all, the spiral comes and goes,
   and in the city it dehisces;
a concise rain washes your brow as you sigh, and the pendulum's arc and the
   moist fountains return the scent to you, the smooth sea-code of dreams.

The edifice of the echo liberates you from all sense;
your serious happiness flows out behind you in an ecstasy of ancient voyage.
A petrifying hand on your cheek, and anxiety, and the epistle and the minerals

make music for the adoring animals who, to the cadence of your laughter and
weeping, name your attire
—and your hair leads you toward absence.

And in those cities—o habitant!—death is strong and manifold, and agony
powerful; dreams surge from your blood
—they reveal the heavenly body of the forgotten letter—the letter missing from
the missing word
—and the luxury of blood spills over into cities where it is not possible to die.

VIII

The water decants a hymn to freeze breath and shadow.
Let your washed head stretch proportion this far, and I'll comb the sides of the sea
and the lost fire glittering in the proud, the dead dampness.

(In the distance of the abyss, abruptly, the night moth turned reflective, invisible,
and patient as the devotion and suppleness radiating from its legs.)
One arrives, hides in not knowing he has arrived, and finds a roaring:
it would seem to be your voice,
but the suddenness of light and the smell of antiquity
conceal the smile of its nascent ecstasy.

X

I glimpse you
—if the beginnings of night have spilled, a glimmering welcomes me.
The moment you cross the blackness, a trumpet blast cancels you;
you are the irremediable sign of the cities and the brilliances.

You are on both shores, in me; in the far weaving you inhabit smoke and hill
and the woven rain resembles what you've abandoned and what I will never
  inhabit.
As soon as sorrow comes, I search for you in my sorrow
—when I was a breath and an arena,
where, what were you doing,
you are inside yourself but in reality you would not be.

You beg me, melancholically, to reshape you as a fountain, black-stockinged
  sorceress, lover, sometimes, of oblivion
—habitant who knows she doesn't exist, who doesn't elude seeingness and
  feelingness:
it's hilarious, that I am and you are not.
Your life without me, it's impossible to consider.

May your voice be present, be forever here,
whether I hear it or not.
Be present, always be.

XI

From the dead one, gazing from sublime heights at the twilight's last shudder,
a faint heat has been left in you,
—the blue form's trace in the firm chord that rocks the wind with faint heat,
it is in you.

May the silence offer a bit of sweetness, break off from forgetfulness
so it might die in a forgetfulness
and dilute itself in you and pass away in the pour of rain;
and may all things be language unfolding at the sign of a sigh.
And may a ship from the skies reveal our flesh and our hurt.

XVI

Don't play that music
—when it gets cold, the forms crave a breath of your grace, a sibilance, a
    descending dew.

The chasm of your weight is moist, and the sphinxes avert their eyes from you;
if what surrounds you is yours and scrubs you clean, you watch, being sphinx
—the surrounding watchfulness radiates from you in the alpha and omega of
    your symphonic life.

I want to discover what wind carries you and what rain, and your vision's essence
    in the country of first causes

—I urge you to come and wake me, astound me.

The night's transience compels and undoes me;

my body is parceled out, and no one is able to see it or to see me.

I lie down—if I sigh, or touch, or look at myself, it all would end: transparency's
    hope,

life itself; the promise of tresses and lights in your apparition

and the welcome of the temples and the greeting of the songs.

My voice acclaims a feat; the furious motion of the black hand writes that your
    avowal is fruitless.

If you don't plan to sleep with the fishes, if you don't utterly change,

the extravagant black music will plunge into water, and the city will flow away in
    a sibilation.

XVII

Sink your lips into shared death, sheltered by the fingers above and below it,

bury yourself in the unargued and unstated, in the half-light of those who die in
    vacillation

—for death comes not just from life, but also through vacillating.

(Death, full and harmonic, has nothing to do with death by vacillation,

and I don't mean that those who don't vacillate might be immortal.)

If you don't pick up a spider's scent and can't read the stillness, you die;

but never if your brow were bitten, only so long as you didn't dream it was your
    own brow biting you.

When you haven't vacillated, death waits for the bite of your brow in order to
   receive you.

Still, love leads me to clamor for your safekeeping in luminous echoes and
   universal tasks,
in active and motionless masses that freeze and proffer joy.
A wild clamor sustains your preservation, your particular time beyond
   temperature's sign.

May my wish be engraved in solemnity, in warmth and in wombness.

Like a Light

In the hour of the star's dying,
my eyes will lock on the firmament that shimmered with you.
Soundlessly and like a light,
lay the transparency of forgetfulness
on my path.

Your breath returns me to the patience and sadness of the earth,
don't divide yourself from evening's fall
—let me see, on the other side of you,
what remains for me to die.

You Are Visible

You stay and stay in the fragrance of the mountains
when the sun goes down,
and it seems to me I can hear your breathing in the freshness of the shade
like a pensive good-bye.

At the threshold of your leaving, firelike, these clear images will yearn for you.
They are rocked here and distantly by the evening's wind;
I accompany you with the rustling of leaves; I watch for you the things you loved
—dawn will not efface your passing; you are visible.

For You

In the furnace of your form my blood flows, in the air of dreaming
you are the weather for aloneness
—a shadow sings in the water's depths for you, to the rhythm of my heart
and in your gaze my eyes are quiet from the music
borne by light's breath
in the sky and in the darkness.

Tonight I gather your form,
the echo of your mouth at the core of a forgotten song
—and I embrace you.

Come

Come; I am nourished by your depiction
and by your redolent melody,
I dreamed of the star that could be reached with a song
—I saw you appear and couldn't grasp you; the song carried you an unsettling
    distance,
and the remoteness was too great and your breath too faint to reach the
    light-burst of my heart in time
—my heart, drowned in a compassionate rain, fiercely efflorescing.

Come, nevertheless; let my hand impress on your forgetting an unforgettable
    force,
draw near to witness my shadow on the wall,
come once; I want to fulfill my passion for good-bye.

Saenz in séance

Aniversario de una visión
(1960)

A la imagen que encendió unos perdidos y
escondidos fuegos.

Saenz as a young man

I

Lo flotante se pierde, y toda la vida se queda en la luz de la primavera que ha
   traído tu mirar
—y mientras perduras en el eco yo contemplo tu partida con el humo en pos del
   horizonte,
y la esperanza y la substancia transparente discurren a lo lejos:
vives la dulzura cuando piensa la hermosura con tristeza tu presencia,
y apareces de medio perfil
al tañido de unos instrumentos nocturnos, azules y dorados, que relumbran, que
   palpitan y que vuelan
en el hueco de mi corazón.

No me atrevo a mirarte por no quedarme dentro de ti, y no te alabo por que no
   pierdas la alegría
—con tu contemplación me contento y tú lo sabes y finges no mirarme
y sueles dar saltos exagerando con una divina profundidad,
como si estuvieras a caballo o en motocicleta
—tu extravagancia me asombra y me regocija, y es mi pan de cada día
—cuando llueve, de tus hombros salen gritos al girar de la cabeza,
y te acaricias las mejillas y das palmadas que resuenan en el agua en el viento y en
   la niebla
—¡cómo te amo me asombra!,
yo te echo de menos a tiempo de escucharte,
una música sepulcral se pierde en el olvido y mi muerte sale de ti,
a los músicos se les aparecen las imágenes amadas
cuando escuchas tú
—todo el tiempo, los músicos se alegran del silencio
cuando escuchas tú.

II

Tu recorrido en las calles te separa de mí, de igual manera que el día y las calles
de por sí
—la ciudad es toda entera una araña que te guarda de mí,
y la luz te incomunica; te aparta, y me hace espiar lo bien que te vigila
—brilla tu júbilo en las esquinas,
a la hora de la desolación yo me pregunto si encontraré el alto azul profundo
de tu vestimenta,
mi país,
el aire de tu voz al caer la tarde
—y me pregunto por qué renunciaría jubilosamente al júbilo que tú me
causas.

Tu parecido a mi no se encuentra en ti, ni en mí, ni tampoco en mi parecido a ti
pero en alguna línea trazada al acaso y que el olvido hizo memorable
—y en el olor que se desprende de ciertos dibujos que nos hacen llorar
y que a la vez nos causan júbilo,
por ser un miedo al sabor de las evocaciones tu visión conmovedora,
aquel suave testimonio que la juventud dejó de su partida:
imagen escondida,
sabor de juventud a la espera de fundirse con la hora de la muerte que es tu
forma que camina con luz y con amor a lo largo de los días y las noches y
los años para lastimar mi corazón
—mi muerte se habrá llevado tu mirar porque sentía dentro de ti cuando la
buscabas,
pues en ti se encubre y permanece;
déjame nombrarte su ropaje,
en ti se quedará la juventud.

III

Tú exageras sin exagerar porque sabes que mis exageraciones hacen que exageres
   tú,
y mis exageraciones son invisibles a fin de que tus exageraciones, no solamente
   por causa de la edad sean visibles;
y de modo tan sutil, yo contribuyo mi grano de arena al descubrimiento de un
   remedio para el mal de amor
—mas, estoy solo y deslumbrado, y necesito socorro frente a este paroxismo de
   exageraciones, las que anuncian algún júbilo caótico
—y no sé si tú eres o si es el demonio quien me deslumbra y me hace ver lo que
   no se ve
y vivir una vida que no es vida ni es sueño, pero miedo, un miedo de soñar en lo
   que mi alma no conoce,
un milagro de dulzura y de verdad transformado en una broma cuando al vuelo
   de una mariposa prorrumpí en una queja
y buscando vida y sentido mis esfuerzos y penurias resultaron siendo un chiste
—pues yo no sabía que tuviésemos que fingir ser otros por ser los mismos;
y no somos como lo que somos ni tampoco parecemos ser lo que somos,
sino que tú y yo seremos, y también yo seré tú y tú serás yo,
tan solamente por medio del fingimiento
—y además, ahora he llegado a saber que el amor no es, sino lo que se oculta en
   el amor;
y para encontrarlo, yo tendré que traspasar lo que creo ser, o sea tú, y llegar a ser
   tú, o sea yo
(en realidad, tú eres porque yo pienso, y eres la verdadera realidad)
—y tú harás de la misma manera,
mas, no suspires, no vayas por acá ni por allá,
pero adonde se mira con fijeza y se suspira de verdad,
y donde un toro iracundo embiste al milagro

que desbautizará para bautizar,
y que de verdad te nombrará—por dentro, y no por fuera.

IV

De haber milagro, no hay tal; y yo clamo por el olvido de la palabra, la unifica-
   ción de los reinos y la comunicación por medio de los ojos, el retorno al alma—
   tú perecerás,
      y nadie habrá visto tu alma, excepto yo;
         y en cambio tú, ni siquiera me ves la cara, y mientras yo reconozco la tuya
            entre muchedumbres,
               cuando no me reconoces crees tú que creo que soy una mosca, y que ignoro
            que te conozco y creo que yo creo lo que tú;
pero, has de saber que si yo fuese en verdad una mosca, aunque me mirases yo no
   sabría a quién miras tú, y te miraría sin sentir ni comprender el por qué
   —y por tanto, si soy como nací, eso se debe al terror, del cual soy hijo; pues no
   era nada imposible nacer como mosca—y de ello no cabe duda, según se ve;
y luego, yo puedo clamar, como que clamo, y buscar remedio a un mal que a mí
   no me aqueja, pero a ti,
alguien que, al creer ser quien no es, me mira, y de tal suerte, como si yo fuera lo
   que él siendo yo,
se mira a sí mismo, pero no a mí, desde que en realidad soy yo el que cree que él
   me mira,
cuando no me mira, por mirarlo yo:
es decir yo soy yo y tú eres tú y te miro y por eso creo que tú me miras, y tú no
   me miras pero crees que lo haces toda vez que tú me miras,
con la diferencia que yo no me miro a mí sino que creo hacerlo por mirarte a ti,
o sea que yo soy yo, y tú no eres tú sino yo;

en una palabra: hay y no hay comunicación; y tú no existes, y yo dejo de existir al
ocuparme de ti, puesto que salgo de mí por que existas tú
—en conclusión, yo te digo que es éste el tono a emplearse cuando de penetrar en
las cuestiones de amor se trata—una cosa oscura,
para cuya explicación el tono apropiado tendrá que ser oscuro, pero no lúcido;
y yo digo que la sensatez tan solamente sirve para explicarse lo que es ella misma,
pues con el tono sensato, en realidad te has abismado en tu propia sensatez cuando
crees haber logrado aclarar lo que querías;
oscuro, muy oscuro deberá de ser el tono, si se quiere hacer desencadenar lo que
el amor oculta;
y habrá de ser muy grande la oscuridad del tono en la iluminación de mi
despedida de ti,
cuando me encuentre un cuerpo sin cuerpo y sin ti, un aerolito por la falta de ti,
sin el silencio de tus ojos, sin la fantasía que iba a revelarme la forma de tus labios
y sin el viaje y la llegada del sueño y de la luz, que ya te envolvían para traerte
por entero junto a mí
   —¡quién sabe, con qué de gestos, con qué de volteretas yo hubiera saludado
   tu aparición encantadora!
   —y mientras que te espero durante muchos años y me contengo de vivir
   y te espero un minuto y vivo aprisa,
   yo quisiera un eclipse de luna para ver cumplirse las ilusiones que me
   quedan de besarte,
   no importaría con la mitad de un beso o sin un beso y en el trance de oscuri-
   dad o de luz
   —y mis esperanzas, bajo tu mirar,
se volverían la verdadera vida que yo miro en el fondo de tus ojos.

V

A la vista del río, que lava de males a los habitantes y los mantiene despiertos,
y que socava la delgada corteza que sostiene a la ciudad debajo de la cual se oculta
   un gran abismo,
no me dirigiré a ti, por un momento y deseo de tenerme en lo que habitas y habita
   en ti—y también en mí,
y percibir la forma, angosta y alargada de la muerte, en la substancia húmeda y
   dura del cristal que le sirve de vivienda,
y conocer la manera de ser y no ser como la muerte, que sabe crecer de arriba
   hacia abajo
—quiero descubrir por qué sentimos que nos movemos, en cuál espacio, en cuál
   sitio, en cuál distancia se mueve el movimiento en la quietud,
donde busca el movimiento un ir de un lugar a otro sin necesidad de ir, y busca
   realizarse en la inmovilidad y dentro de sí mismo,
      como la superficie de este río y como sus aguas, discurriendo lentamente
         junto con nosotros,
      para desembocar en el mar, para hundirnos y salvarnos de no morir por la
         ausencia de la muerte,
      la que un instante atrás ignoraba nuestra vida,
      la que viaja en ellas ahora y se aleja de nuestro lado.

¡Pasa sordo y ruidoso el río!—se desliza y salta a través de los diques,
   a su estruendo se enardecen las visiones de grandes animales
   que vemos cuando a solas nos desahogamos de cierta rara tristeza,
   en la transparencia y en el olvido de los suspiros que el río eleva y pro-
      fundiza en medio de emanaciones mefíticas,
   y al silbido del aire puro que el Illimani ha filtrado,
   y que sopla sobre lo turbio e impetuoso de nuestra inclinación,

esas visiones se debaten entre suspiros y buscan en lo tumultuoso de las
        aguas alguna visión que las mire y suspire por ellas,
—y, mientras respiramos el extracto de este gran aire, filtrado, azul y frío,
a la hora de las sombras, con una turbadora penetración las emanaciones mefíticas
        nos transportan al mar,
y nos diluyen en la redondez de la tierra y en una eminencia del cielo
        —yo te busco,
        y con el alba y con los suspiros,
        junto al claro de las estrellas se anima la ciudad
        —y pasa el río, desconsoladamente y se queda.

VI

En las pródigas luces humedecidas
y en los aires de navegación de las montañas,
en las solitarias inmensidades de la limpidez y en las humaredas, al calor fugitivo
        de la grave curvatura del mundo
        —en las calles y en los árboles,
la lluvia refleja la callada ternura de tu visión.

Y de las tumbas un suspiro enciende perdidos y escondidos fuegos
        en tu sentida imagen,
        a la ascensión de aquel melancólico vaho desde las oscuridades,
        que ha resquebrajado los sudarios de tus rumorosos antepasados
—y en las entrañas del agua, al compás que escucho del olvido, llueve,
y llueve y yo no te miro, en realidad puedo mirar que me miras tú,

—¡cómo me miras!,
de unos confines, de la infancia
y de los mares profundos de la juventud
—¡me miras en el vacío y a través de la distancia,
cómo llega tu mirar, de tanta lejanía y en qué conmovida manera,
que me hace saber que yo no te miro!
—y un gran llanto me sacude al deseo de encontrarte,
y hablar contigo sobre la gratitud, sobre la primavera y la alegría
y sobre cosas tantas y diversas,
y a un tiempo te escucho—en la huella que ha quedado en mi frente, en una
  sombra que roza la pared—,
te escucho hablar de todo cuanto me hace llorar
—y así respondes a lo que digo en mi corazón.

VII

Que sea larga tu permanencia bajo el fulgor de las estrellas,
  yo dejo en tus manos mi tiempo
  —el tiempo de la lluvia
  perfumará tu presencia resplandeciente en la vegetación.

Renuncio al júbilo, renuncio a ti: eres tú el cuerpo de mi alma; quédate
  —yo he transmontado el crepúsculo y la espesura, a la apacible luz de tus
  ojos
  y me interno en la tiniebla;
  a nadie mires,
  no abras la ventana. No te muevas:

hazme saber el gesto que de tu boca difunde silenciosa la brisa;
estoy en tu memoria, hazme saber si tus manos me acarician
y si por ellas el follaje respira
—hazme saber de la lluvia que cae sobre tu escondido cuerpo,
y si la penumbra es quien lo esconde o el espíritu de la noche.

Hazme saber, perdida y desaparecida visión, qué era lo que guardaba tu
mirar
—si era el ansiado y secreto don,
que mi vida esperó toda la vida a que la muerte lo recibiese.

De Al pasar un cometa

(1970–1972)

En lo alto de la ciudad oscura

Una noche en una calle bajo la lluvia en lo alto de la ciudad oscura
con el ruido a lo lejos
es seguro que suspirará
yo suspiraré
tomados de las manos por un gran tiempo en el interior de la arboleda
sus ojos claros al pasar un cometa
—su cara llegada del mar sus ojos en el cielo mi voz dentro de su voz
su boca en forma de manzana su cabello en forma de sueño
una mirada nunca vista en cada pupila
sus pestañas en forma de luz un torrente de fuego
todo será mío dando volteretas de alegría
me cortaré una mano por cada suspiro suyo me sacaré un ojo por cada sonrisa
      suya
me moriré una vez dos veces tres veces cuatro veces mil veces
hasta morir en sus labios
con un serrucho me cortaré las costillas para entregarle mi corazón
con una aguja sacaré a relucir mi mejor alma para darle una sorpresa
los viernes por la tarde
con el aire de la noche cantando una canción me propongo vivir trescientos años
en su hermosa compañía.

Tu calavera
A Silvia Natalia Rivera

Estas lluvias,
yo no sé por qué me harán amar un sueño que tuve, hace muchos años,

con un sueño que tuviste tú
—se me aparecía tu calavera,

Y tenía un alto encanto;
no me miraba a mí—te miraba a ti.
Y se acercaba a mi calavera, y yo te miraba a ti.
Y cuando tú me mirabas a mí, se te aparecía mi calavera;
no te miraba a ti.
Me miraba a mí.

En la alta noche,
alguien miraba;
y yo soñaba tu sueño
—bajo una lluvia silenciosa,
tú te ocultabas en tu calavera,
y yo me ocultaba en ti.

Aquí

En la distancia, en el silencio, en los reinos de la infancia,
alguien lloraba por mí.
Tu antigua mirada ocupaba el espacio, y la eternidad renacía, y la juventud.
Una gota de agua, en lugar de mí.

En la altura

Te miré de cerca, era propicia la primavera en la altura.
Era visible el resplandor en tus entrañas, la revelación de mi afecto por ti,
su causa y secreto
—y cayó la noche.

La canasta de lana

Queriendo sin poder me soñaba en este cuarto durmiendo y me soñaba pudiendo,
haciendo sonar una canasta de lana para quedarme durmiendo,
y queriendo que vengan que no vengan y que hagan que no hagan sonar una
    canasta de lana haciendo un daño sin querer,
ilustrando una música japonesa que me hace llorar recordando mas no
    escuchando,
evocando una escena inevocable que por pura suerte puede evocarse,
como quien dice:
ahora que esta señora evoca hablando y aquel señor habla evocando,
como quien dice:
"Ven aquí, lora; hagamos sonar esta canasta de lana," quedando todos contentos
    con esta música japonesa que me hace llorar evocando,
y que sigue ilustrando y sigue sonando y sigue tocando toda la noche.

Según estoy persuadido

A Jaime Taborga V.

Todos viven en uno
—yo, tú, ellos.
Todos vivimos en todos, nadie vive ni muere, y cada cual se está por su lado
—pero nadie sabe lo que pasa.
El mundo es una conjetura, según estoy persuadido.
La forma que te atribuyes tú o la que yo me atribuyo es la que él asume.
Movimiento y forma son una y misma cosa, y no hay tal redondez del mundo,
pero sí una forma que incesantemente se transforma en virtud de los movimientos
    del tiempo,
los cuales ya se comprimen ya se expanden en las espirales, en las esencias y en las
    existencias, o en los reinos del caos,
para retornar a la partícula primordial, o para alejarse hacia las regiones de lo
    increado y lo no creado,
en donde nada pasa por más que pase, y en donde todo pasa por más que no pase;
debiendo de encontrarse precisamente allí la causa última de la forma,
según estoy persuadido.

La ciudad

A Blanca Wiethüchter y Ramiro Molina

Con el humo y con el fuego, mucha gente apagada y silenciosa,
en una calle, en una esquina,
en la alta ciudad, contemplando el futuro en busca del pasado
—en las entrañas sutiles el relámpago nocturno,
en el ojo caviloso, las meditaciones se vuelven agonía.

En otra época, la esperanza y la alegría servían para algo—era invisible el paso
  del tiempo,
y la oscuridad, una cosa invisible,
tan sólo revelada a los infinitos ancianos avanzando a tientas que procuran
  palparte para saber si entre ellos no estás tú,
mientras procuran palpar a unos niños a quienes creen palpar, no obstante que
  éstos los palpan a ellos y se confunden con ellos a tiempo de palparte a ti,
palpando a solas un manto de oscuridad que fue tejido con una tristeza sin límites
  por algún habitante,
muerto y perdido en esta oscuridad transparente que es la ciudad en que
  actualmente habito yo,
habitando una ciudad en el fondo de mi alma que no habita sino tan sólo un
  habitante
—y tal una ciudad llena de chispas, llena de estrellas, llena de fuegos en las
  esquinas,
llena de carbones y de ascuas en los aires,
tal una ciudad en que muchos seres solitarios y alejados de mí, se mueven y mur-
  muran con un destino que el cielo ya no sabe,
con unos ojos, con unos ídolos, y con unos niños que ese mismo cielo arrebató,
sin más vida que la vida, sin más tiempo que el tiempo,
amurallados en las grandes paredes del fuego y del olvido, mecidos en el vaivén
  de las desesperanzas,
llorando calladamente con esta ciudad que se hunde.

Y ningún ángel o demonio en este pozo de silencio.
Solamente los fuegos a lo largo de las calles.
Solamente los contornos helados de las sombras, la calma de un sol que se retira.
El soplo de un alba que por última vez amaneció, el chirrido de las puertas con el
  viento,

los ámbitos que estallan y que se dispersan, y las formas que se funden con las
   llamas,
los signos y los cantos,
con una angustia muy recóndita, en el suelo y más allá del suelo,
y la respiración de los muertos, las lluvias incesantes,
el abandono con sabor de pan, en una casa que entre sueños me persigue,
los patios y las gradas, los seres y las piedras, y los corredores infinitos;
las ventanas que se abren al vacío y se cierran al espanto,
los cuartos en que me pierdo y los rincones en que me oculto
—las lóbregas paredes y el húmedo musgo, los confines en los cuales busco no sé
   qué,
ocultándome del vasto olor de las costumbres.

Ninguna voz, ninguna luz, ningún testimonio de mi antigua vida.
Solamente los fuegos,
inextinguibles aunque siempre menguantes, y tan solamente los fuegos.
El desolado portento del fantasma que una vez se llamó la juventud
—en mi ciudad, en mi morada.

Mirando cómo pasa el río

A Leonardo García-Pabón

Llegada la hora hablaré contigo, mirando cómo pasa el río, al lado del río.
Con el perfil de tu frente, con el eco de tu voz, difundiendo mi voz en lo
   profundo,
en las grandes amplitudes en las cuales el ojo de la muerte ha mirado, conocerás la
   palabra oculta.

Donde el viento permanece. Donde el vivir se acaba y donde el color es uno y
solo.

Donde el agua no se toca, y donde la tierra no se toca: donde tú sabes estar, en mi
estar invisible,

en estado milenario

—de obras, de olores y de formas; de animales, de minerales, de vegetales en el
tiempo.

En el tiempo del tiempo. En la raíz del presentimiento. En la semilla, en la angustia,
solamente tú conocerás la palabra oculta.

La soledad del mundo. La soledad del hombre. La razón de ser del hombre y del
mundo

—la soledad circular de la esfera. El crecimiento

y el decrecimiento;

el cierre de la cosa hermética. El cierre hermético de la cosa.

El ingente, el incalculable—el inconmensurable sepulcro indiviso y vacío.

Alguien tendrá que llamarse crepúsculo

A Carlos Ramírez

Persiste el resplandor a lo largo de los años.

Persiste el horizonte en que resuenan y en que se apagan mis pasos conforme
discurre el crepúsculo.

Las lluvias de primavera, la espera que comienza cuando el año se acaba, y la
visión que siempre aparece;

este cielo de duendes, este cielo de cosas y de sombras; persiste el caer de la tarde.

Persisten los muertos, las piedras y los cantos; las nubes y los ruidos y las vidas;

la oscuridad, el mundo y la distancia.

Persiste el resplandor a lo largo de los años.

Pues no puede consumirse sino la verdadera vida que vive del resplandor que la consume.

Muchas veces al buscar sin poder encontrarte el crepúsculo me sorprendía a la hora de tus ojos.

Muchas veces me olvidé de ti, quise olvidarme y recordar, y recordé que tenía que olvidarte,

acordándome de ti por lo mismo que no quería recordarte

—el crepúsculo me envolvía en tales circunstancias, perfectamente lo recuerdo.

Yo te confundía con el crepúsculo al confundirme contigo;

tú me confundías con el crepúsculo al confundirte conmigo,

y tú y yo nos confundíamos con el crepúsculo, que nos confundía a ti conmigo y a mí contigo,

confundiéndose contigo el confundido conmigo, para confundirse conmigo el confundido contigo.

Y muchas veces se confundían en una y misma persona el crepúsculo y tú y yo,

y otras muchas cada cual se confundía con otras tres personas distintas,

que con esto se volvían nueve en total, o sea cero.

Y no había tal persona llamada crepúsculo,

sino que en realidad no había persona que no se llamara crepúsculo,

excepto las llamadas tú y yo, que sin embargo no podían dejar de llamarse crepúsculo.

De El escalpelo (1955)

Homenaje a la epilepsia

ESTOS SON CABELLOS DEL PEQUEÑO EPILÉPTICO

Los cabellos del pequeño epiléptico se distienden tenebrosos en los albores de la noche. Mueven sus resinas con términos acompasados, y parecen gigantescas columnas de granito en el glorioso y misterioso ámbito del amor y de la muerte.

En estos cabellos, a los que respeto porque son personas, hay columpios de inexplicable redondez, en los cuales veo la negrura mágica y amada del espacio.

Son los cabellos del muerto en la irradiación de una mano que ha metido sus dedos en el misterio.

EL COCHE DE MUERTOS

Hace mucho tiempo, cuando yo era niño, trataron de enseñarme cosas acerca de ciertas cosas. Pero no logré aprender normas acerca de la disciplina.

Un día caminaba ante la ciudad y vi un coche. Me causó mucha tristeza. No sé, ahora, si era verde, o azul, o rojo, pero durante el transcurso de mi vida llegué a la conclusión de que no tenía color, y que simplemente era un coche.

Ese coche que vi un día de mi infancia había yo estado inficionado de no sé qué fuerzas extrañas y no sé de qué extraños conocimientos.

Era el coche de muertos, de acuerdo a lo que me revelara años después el niño epiléptico, a quien encontré en un día de sol . . .

Este acontecimiento, desde luego, carece de importancia, pese a que el niño llama a un coche cualquiera, "coche de muertos."

UN MUERTO SE HA MUERTO

Los muertos, tal como los vivos, también pueden morir otra vez.

Tal la revelación del niño epiléptico, durante una tarde de sol.

Los muertos tienen la capacidad de morirse.

El hecho de morir no le priva a uno del derecho de morir otra vez. Ahí está el secreto de la existencia.

Es por eso que los muertos se han muerto.

Por eso es también que, en cierto modo, los muertos son precoces.

LA PUERTA QUE DA INGRESO AL MISTERIO

Es posible fabricar una puerta, pero no una puerta para que ingresen a una habitación antigua los niños, sino una puerta auténtica para poder ingresar al misterio.

Fabricar un preámbulo de locura, de tal modo que todos los fabricantes de la nada no sepan qué hacer.

Ese niño, estoy seguro, posee los secretos de alguna puerta que puede conducir al misterio, sin recurrir, pongo en claro, a las irremediables putrefacciones.

Hay una puerta. Esa puerta está abierta para ti, para mí, para todos. Está abierta para las ratas, que te contemplan noche tras noche desde la luna.

Hay que dejar que ese niño siga con un poco de la puerta del misterio y entregarle algo de sus cabellos antes que desconozca los caminos y las piedras.

(Es ahí donde reside el secreto de la puerta.)

UN FÓSFORO APAGADO

Un fósforo apagado es simplemente un fósforo apagado. Lo trascendente del fósforo apagado es que está apagado, y que, pese a que ya no es, se le llame fósforo.

Pero ese fósforo que está allí, sobre una hoja de papel, está muerto. Eso sí que es importante. Porque lo importante es que esté muerto.

Es el ser, y hay que verlo, allí, tan substancial como el universo. Como cosa que se integra en las etapas de la nada.

SUDARIO QUE RESGUARDA PAPELES CORTADOS

Es un sudario. Estoy seguro que todos han visto un sudario en su niñez, aunque sea por escrito. Han visto todos en su niñez sudarios y sudarios. Sin embargo, yo he comenzado a congelar los sudarios del mundo.

De pronto retorno a mi vivienda. Veo un sudario limpio y fresco, pero eso es en broma solamente.

Duermo en sábanas apagadas y lunares, y sueño con los sudarios.

Me cubren, sujetan quedamente mi próxima podredumbre, rechinan sus teas sobre mi cuerpo glorioso en medio de la noche oscura. Luego, en la magia, adquieren vida para envolverme con los animales del destino.

Son papeles cortados por la luna. Hay que dejarlos allí, donde duermen las mesas vulnerables, todos, todos, las arañas vulnerables, hay que dejarlos tal como están, con la música, de sus sudarios de niño.

Los papeles cortados van por el mundo con la llaga melancólica de los adioses.

EL ALARIDO PROFUNDO

Es solamente un alarido profundo. Viene de lejos. Nada tiene que ver con el vientre, ni con los pulmones o el hígado. Es, llanamente, un alarido ante el cual uno quiere irse, apaciblemente, a la luna, llevando ciertos cabellos de cierto niño profundo. "Un alarido profundo tiene que ser siempre," me han dicho, "el alarido, de la humanidad."

IMAGEN DEL NIÑO

Su imagen es dulce. Nadie puede verla, excepto el caracol que anida a sus pies a orillas del mar.

Nadie puede verla, excepto las arañas que moran donde moras tú y donde moran las memorables máquinas orgánicas de la eternidad.

Nada puede detener su deseo de niñez.

Es así su imagen. La vida de las imágenes ilusorias de la muerte y de la vida.

Tiene él un esquema.

Ese esquema es la reseña del secreto del amor y de la muerte, aunque el niño ignore amor y muerte, aunque sea vaga omnipotencia en medio de este juicio para practicar homenaje a la epilepsia.

(Objeto muerto y puro para recoger la soledad.)

Concluye ahora todo. La catástrofe es bella.

Aquí, en medio de la noche, acabo de rendir homenaje al misterioso epiléptico, así, con tanta mansedumbre como una laguna.

Rindo mi homenaje. Calladamente, viene la catástrofe. Los alfileres apuntan al cielo. Será así siempre.

Los ojos se tornan amarillos, y se connaturalizan con otras cosas que no son. Ya viene la verdadera vida.

Paráfrasis de "¿Y le has dicho? ¿O no?"

La paráfrasis de lo que había dicho se parece a Wiesbaden. Con lo lluviosa y fugitiva que es, con lo clara que es, y con esa capacidad súbita que tiene para mezclarse entre el tumulto, luego de pasar a cinco centímetros de mí, sin apenas conocerme, o como si nos hubiésemos conocido alguna vez en la orilla de algún mar profundo, con lana en el fondo, y, en la superficie, con peces ardientes, ahuecados hacia la espalda y la columna vertebral un poco rígida. Peces con la maravillosa capacidad de individualizar. Te llaman por tu nombre, aunque no lo creas. Contrariamente a los otros géneros de peces, pueden girar sus pupilas para seguir tus movimientos, y pueden (este es un extraño caso de devoción) salir del mar y arrastrarse arenas arriba, hasta perecer, solamente por cumplir su función, que es la de seguirte por entre la multitud rabiosa y enloquecida que nada busca.

Pero, entendido está, tú no eres la multitud. Tú, más bien, eres la esencia, el ser de la multitud. Se entiende que la multitud dimana de ti, y se entiende hasta la congoja que no habría multitud de no ser tú. Es por eso que yo amo no solamente a la multitud, sino a las multitudes. La amo y las amo porque tengo un concepto tuyo amplísimo de eternidad, y porque el primigenio clima para conocer algún estrecho pasadizo de lo angustioso consiste en la multitud, y en las multitudes, a la cual y a las cuales has dado vida tú con el maravilloso enigma de la palabra dicha y escuchada desde el ámbito de pocos centímetros: "¿Y le has dicho? ¿O no?"

Esto que estoy haciendo, y que llamo "Paráfrasis de '¿Y le has dicho? ¿O no?' " no es más que una incidencia, de viejas, remotas conjeturas, de negras, feroces y lúcidas ensoñaciones acerca de ti, cuando alguna vez tenía yo, (yo, yo mismo) los brazos al viento, el olor, digamos, de Wiesbaden—como esta tarde— y la calavera fresca.

La vela y el viento (Fragmento)

Hay un hombre metido en el fuego, en tanto que otro observa su desventura desde los bordes del agua sin acometer la idea de la llama en que se debate la vela moribunda y distante de las realidades en que se torna plato o riñón la tierra, o en que un tomate pueda dar la sensación del color claro y rosado, para identificarse con los ardores de garganta que tienen los niños, sean bellos, sean víctimas de la viruela o hábiles equilibristas.

Por ventura, acaso tú no has visto alguna vez el núcleo de la llama, y no te has espantado ante su maravilla. Acaso no has pensado alguna vez en los ardores de las manos, en los ardores del cuello, en los del convento al amanecer, cuando uno busca algo que se parezca a una piedra bendita para comérsela; no has pensado acaso en la escarlatina del niñito, de ése, cuajado de bosques, inmerso en la melancolía, alegórico y fino, desmenuzado por la tormenta, suave de jabón, intrínsicamente blando, con su nuca alargada y sus labios monstruosos, y la camisa hecha pedazos, con un olor de flores en los hombros y en las rodillas.

Hay, en su actitud, una vela sobrenatural, que da la medida del destino. Hay sobre todo una minúscula aguja sobre su traje, que da la medida del fuego y del viento.

Si ves un incendio, te acuerdas de ella. Si ves el mar, te acuerdas de ella; y si ves los núcleos terrosos de los anchos y secos caminos, te acuerdas de ella.

Hay un lapso de rocas y de algarabías cuando tú prendes una vela para dar cierta alegoría a su muerte, tan minúscula, tan triste, lluviosa y redondeada por el fuego.

E.

"E"; sabes tú qué significa "E."

"E" significa la muerte primera, la única muerte, la de uno, para que los otros se queden horriblemente solos y orgullosos de vivir y de lavarse con jabones finos.

Eso quiere decir "E." "E," tan muerta y silenciosa y arquitectónica como la vives ahora, para usarla o no y decir "estoy," "una," "era," "espanto," "espero," "enagua," "Caquiaviri," "entonces," "Erasmo," o para decir: "escolar," "estamos yendo a la casa de mi padre," "estoy yo para invitarles alfajores," "ensueño," "no le hagan cosquillas a ningún señor en el colectivo," "parece que se empeñan en no guardar las correas en su lugar," "ranuras," "todavía no han salido los rosquetes del horno," "hay unos hermanos que quieren vender su cafetería, pero al contado," "la ropa está mojada," "siempre quieres salir con la tuya," "alcantarilla."

Así es la "E."

Lo atronador y curioso, lo mismo que la lluvia, es que no puedes aplicar tú la "E" o la "T" a ninguna otra letra del abecedario, y tampoco a la vela o al viento.
La vela y el viento son seres aparte. Incomprensibles. De esta incomprensión dimana tu tristeza. Es la incompatibilidad de tu alma con la vela y el viento.
Andate ahora a dormir con las cosas oscuras que siempre buscas y no encuentras.

El viaje de los tilos y las madréporas cuando se reside en el cansancio de las viejas cunas (Fragmento)

Caminan en el eco. Caminan oscuramente, como caminan los trances. Caminan desacompasadamente, caminan con esos y angustiosos silbatos nocturnos, portando su alarido, así, mensajeros encumbrados. Caminan con las nalgas, con el pubis olvidado. Pero sobre todo, caminan tan rotundamente que da espanto.

No lo olvides. Caminan forcejeando su ser, caminan como si otro los llevara, caminan terroríficos, plenos, ahuecados, fervorosos.

Caminan como nadie camina. Siguen caminando, acostados a la vera de alguien. Caminan despiertos y dormidos, caminan al revés, caminan a destiempo, frecuentados por raros privilegios.

Caminan como si alguien les dijera: *"No camines."*

(Con el imán a cuestas, saben y no saben hacia donde caminan. Pero eso les lleva a la tormentosa, formidable esencia de aquellas sonrisas olvidadas en el plan del río, en el eco que hace no sé cómo el piano y el chelo, en el clímax de un atardecer frío y deslumbrante. Inevitablemente había de caer la noche.)

Son los inventores de los ruidos, tú lo sabes. Se despiden con un ruido; con un sutil, amargo ruido.

Llevan sus migajas al agua de mar con ruido, y se levantan, y se acuestan, y aparecen con ruido, con el irónico, placentero, profético ruido que hacen los adioses. Son formidables.

Son la forma misteriosa del llanto. Han urdido, sin saberlo, las sabias maneras, oblicuas, universales, eternas. Las sabias maneras del escondido ritmo, del entrañable estruendo con que uno despierta. Las sabias, mágicas maneras del presentimiento, las nobles maneras del círculo y del cuadrado, las maneras extrañas, invisibles, del paradójico ademán, del éxtasis vertido, de la congoja vertida, de la súplica interna, del dolido viaje que fulmina.

Son los descubridores de la melancolía. Son, con su callado terror, precursores de la forma del viaje. Del modo de desplazarse sin nadie ni ellos.

Son vagas y concretas formas, ángeles bestiales, supremos, presuntos, verdaderos, catastróficos, ideales símbolos. Son buenos y silentes, y son, esta noche, universos estupendos, colosales llamados de la nada, vertidos gritos óseos, inolvidables compulsores de tu sonrisa.

Recorrer esta distancia (1973)

A la imagen de Puraduralubia

I

Estoy separado de mí por la distancia en que yo me encuentro;
el muerto está separado de la muerte por una gran distancia.
Pienso recorrer esta distancia descansando en algún lugar.
De espaldas en la morada del deseo,
sin moverme de mi sitio—frente a la puerta cerrada,
con una luz del invierno a mi lado.

En los rincones de mi cuarto, en los alrededores de la silla.
Con la indecisa memoria que se desprende del vacío
—en la superficie del tumbado,
el muerto deberá comunicarse con la muerte.

Contemplando los huesos sobre la tabla, contando las oscuridades con mis dedos a
    partir de ti.
Mirando que se estén las cosas, yo deseo.
Y me encuentro recorriendo una gran distancia.

II

Como el aire nocturno la fiesta del espíritu ya es cosa acabada,
Como la escalera que sobre un muro se apoya para escuchar la palabra es cosa
    acabada.
Como la línea que una vez dibujé y con tu sombra dejaste es cosa acabada.

Como el humo en los braseros con el incienso y con los vapores que se difunden, echando de menos las voces,
como las luces y los espejos que ascienden hacia los cielos de invierno,

con el olvido de las costumbres y de los seres definitivamente distantes en la distancia,
así las cosas y las calaveras ya no son cosas ni calaveras,
en las ceremonias de invierno ya no se usan.

III

Al contacto del secreto que fluye, del tiempo que se detiene, del fuego que se consume, y del hielo eterno y presente,
todo ojo, toda imagen, arderá en llamas y se quemará.
Toda concavidad en el seno de la tierra, toda oscuridad que descienda, se quedará para siempre.
(Si eres brujo, ríete. Mas si no lo fueses, y te dicen que el diablo te persigue, no te rías.)
Con los años que discurren y los giros de estos mundos y las luces recibidas contemplando las estrellas puedo darme cuenta de las cosas.
Toda alma se diluye en las aguas torrenciales con el alma universal.

IV

Los grandes malestares causados por las sombras, las visiones melancólicas surgidas de la noche,

todo lo horripilante, todo lo atroz, lo que no tiene nombre, lo que no tiene porqué,
hay que soportarlo, quien sabe por qué.

Si no tienes qué comer sino basura, no digas nada.
Si la basura te hace mal, no digas nada.
Si te cortan los pies, si te queman las manos, si la lengua se te pudre, si te partes la
    espalda, si te rompes el alma, no digas nada.
Si te envenenan no digas nada, aunque se te salgan las tripas por la boca y se te
    paren los pelos de punta; aunque se aneguen tus ojos en sangre, no digas nada.
Si te sientes bien no te sientas bien. Si te quedas no te quedes. Si te mueres no te
    mueras. Si te apenas no te apenes. No digas nada.
Vivir es difícil; cosa difícil no decir nada.
Soportar a la gente sin decir nada no es nada fácil.
Es muy difícil—en cuanto pretende que se la entienda sin decir nada,
entender a la gente sin decir nada.
Es terriblemente difícil y sin embargo muy fácil ser gente;
pero es lo difícil no decir nada.

V

El odio que el padre que es hijo profesa al hijo que es padre, es padre del odio que
    el hijo que es padre profesa al padre que es hijo.
Todos conspiran contra todos y se muerden y se despedazan los unos a los otros;
    jamás se mueren de hambre y comen caca, coman o no coman caca, comercien
    o no comercien con sedas y licores y toda clase de mercaderías,

se ríen del género humano y tallan diamantes, dejan de tallar y se ponen a jugar,
    ya al dominó, ya a las carreras, ya a las apuestas, toda clase de juegos,
van al campo y navegan a su gusto, viajan en tren, vuelan en avión, comen bizco-
    chos y reparten besos y saludos,
muy ufanos de sus zapatos bien lustrados, de sus cabellos cortados a la última
    moda, de su tez bien asoleada, y de sus carteras de cuero de cocodrilo.
Se ponen pensativos leyendo los periódicos, suspiran con moderación, tosen con
    suficiencia, y caen enfermos de vez en cuando, con la distinción con que las
    normas lo prescriben;
y hay que ver el tono que se dan cuando suben al avión.
El aire majestuoso que suelen adoptar cuando hablan de tecnología, la severidad
    de su lenguaje cuando hablan de moral,
la elegancia y despreocupación con que se suenan las narices, esa leve inclinación
    de la cabeza, esa simpatía, ese no sé qué, con que sonríen,
hay que ver ese raro don de gentes, el empuje, la drasticidad, el talento, el secreto
    encanto que en todos sus actos demuestran,
y la espiritualidad del gesto; esa desconcertante sutileza con que opinan sobre arte
    y psicología;
el criterio sabio y la versación acerca del dolor humano, y con qué congoja dan su
    veredicto;
hay que ver la grandeza soberana en la mirada con que suelen perdonar los erro-
    res de los miserables mortales;
la consumada técnica con que mascan y con que tragan las mil vitaminas para
    mantenerse rollizos y proteger la salud;
la elegancia con que acuden a consultar al psiquiatra, a tiempo de mirar el reloj y
    ponerse nerviosos—un poco nerviosos, no demasiado, con rictus aristocrático
    y nobleza en la frente;
hay que ver la gallardía con que se mueven en el mundo y la importancia que se
    atribuyen en la vida;

la significación trascendental en cada uno de sus ademanes, y, más aún, en cada
uno de sus tics nerviosos, por más que no tengan ninguno;
hay que ver las heroicas actitudes, el timbre de ferocidad que imprimen a la voz,
la tremenda osadía en sus determinaciones cuando se mueren de susto, el temblor
en el upiti cuando se hielan de espanto,
y los ayes y los íes, los oyes y los úyes, con que claman socorro, en cuanto creen
ver amenazadas sus preciadas existencias por algún fantasma,
y las paradas de gallo viejo con que pretenden ocultar el terror que los domina;
hay que ver lo que todavía les espera con cierto demonio cobrando forma dentro
de ti,
que los reventará sin asco, gracias a tu mutismo y por obra de tu mutismo.

VI

Presiento un lóbrego día, un espacio cerrado, un suceder incomprensible, una
noche interminable como la inmortalidad.
Lo que presiento no tiene nada que ver conmigo, ni contigo; no es cosa personal,
no es cosa particular lo que presiento;
pero tiene que ver con no sé qué
—tal vez con el mundo, o con los reinos del mundo, o con los misteriosos encan-
tos del mundo;
se puede mirar a través de las aguas una profunda fisura.
Se puede percibir, por el olor de las cosas y por las formas que ellas asumen, el
cansancio de las cosas.
En lo que crece, en lo que ha dejado de crecer, en lo que resuena, en lo que per-
manece, en lo que no permanece, en el aire silencioso, en las evoluciones del
insecto, en los árboles que murmuran,

se puede adivinar el júbilo de un próximo acabamiento.

Las oscuridades devoradoras, ansiosas de devorar fenecido el término, ya nada
será.

Tal vez una brizna, en lo alto de algún lugar, tal vez en lo profundo de algún lugar,
flotando en las últimas aguas.

El resuello, sin principio ni fin, una envoltura para la inmovilidad,
envolviendo el movimiento del circulo que se repite
—no sé explicar, no sé decir en qué consiste el presentimiento que presiento.

VII

En el extraño sitio en que precisamente la perdición y el encuentro han ocurrido,
la hermosura de la vida es un hecho que no se puede ni se debe negar.

    La hermosura de la vida,

    por el milagro de vivir.

    La hermosura de la vida,

    que se queda,

    por el milagro de morir.

Fluye la vida, pasa y vuela, se retuerce en una interioridad inalcanzable.

En el aura de los seres que transitan, que se hace perceptible con un latido,
en el viento que vibra con el ir y venir de los seres,
en los decires, en los clamores, en los gritos, en el humo
—en las calles, con una luz en las paredes, unas veces, y otras veces, con una
sombra.

En ese mirar las cosas, con que suelen mirar los animales;

en ese mirar del humano, con que el humano suele mirar el mirar del animal que
    mira las cosas.
En la hechura de la tela,
en el hierro que el hierro es hierro.
En la mesa,
en la casa.
En la orilla del río.
En la humedad del ambiente.
En el calor del verano, en el frío del invierno, en la luz de la primavera
—en un abrir y cerrar de ojos.
Rasgando el horizonte o sepultándose en el abismo,
aparece y desaparece la verdadera vida.

VIII

En un trasfondo hirviente y vibrante echo de menos el encanto.
En el antiguo silencio de un aire echo de menos el encanto.
En el aislado mundo del que nada fluye, como no sea el perdido encanto, lo que
    me remite a ti,
echo de menos la horca en que una vez me viera suspendido para mirarte con
    totalidad,
en todos tus movimientos y pasos
—echo de menos los años, las fechas, los días precisos que se llaman hoy,
los precisos instantes que se llaman ahora—el mañana que ha sido, el ayer que ha
    de ser,
echo de menos algún dolor que era tuyo, que se reunía con algún dolor que era
    mío,

que se adentraba en lo profundo de tus ojos

—en lo profundo de tus ojos, en que echo de menos lo profundo de tus ojos.

IX

Con tinieblas y piruetas portentosas emergen los malabaristas de la noche.

A patadas y codazos se abren paso por entre la multitud de anonadados personajes
    que miran deslumbrados,

sorpresivamente se sitúan en el centro del redondel y ofrecen numerosos malabares.

Se ajustan el cinturón y se revuelcan, con el tropel de caballos enanos que acaban
    de hacer su aparición, guiñan los ojos y no acaban de revolcarse,

y beben café y comen manzanas, hacen esto, hacen lo otro y lo de más allá,

y es esto lo que hacen, y lo otro y lo de más allá, y no otra cosa, hasta que alguien
    entrando en escena resuena,

y comiendo ajos el pitazo resuena,

y todos se encogen y todos se inclinan, y se recogen sobre sí mismos y se
    ensimisman,

en medio del profundo silencio reinante, se encienden las luces, no se encienden
    las luces, se apagan las luces,

al conjuro de los perros brujos que irrumpen en el redondel con espectaculares
    volteretas,

la incertidumbre desciende y luego no desciende con los perros brujos,

que comienzan a trotar en toda la redondez del redondel con gran finura de estilo,
    para salvar obstáculos ya de por sí insalvables,

con gráciles contorsiones y con adecuados y parsimoniosos movimientos,

muy conscientes de la admirable admiración con que los admiradores admirados
    los admiran,

con miles y miles de ojos que ansiosamente se tuercen y se retuercen en las vueltas
    y revueltas de un aparato en verdad aparatoso,
de difícil trayectoria, intrincado de verdad pero no disparatado.
Y con el polvo que levantan, y con el aserrín que levantan, y con los caballos que
    levantan, y con los malabaristas que levantan, y con la basura que levantan, y
    con los enanos que estos perros brujos levantan,
una señora, de hermosura nunca vista se levanta, y, después de sacarse los ojos y
    limpiar sus anteojos, luego de lanzar un grito se desmaya,
y todo es algarabía, todo es exaltación, chocolate y alegría, en alborozados
    corazones, al son del regocijo general,
al ton con que estos perros brujos se levantan, en son de sacarse los ojos, en ton
    de limpiar sus anteojos, en son de dar un grito y desmayarse, sin ton ni son, al
    son de universal consternación,
al ton con que un lebrel sale de quicio, en son de ponerse a ladrar, en ton de
    saltar, en son de ganar la pared, en ton de encaramarse en el poste sustentador
    de los lebreles, en son de irse con éstos,
en ton de internarse en un mundo incierto y no conocido, hostil, cubierto de
    abrojos y exento de margaritas,
en son de desentenderse de un hombre terrestre, tan generoso, tan dadivoso, tan
    cariñoso,
que los contempla con ira impotente y que profiere bufido potente,
con patéticos gestos de asombro, con miradas de poderoso magnetismo,
con cuello de toro y cuernos de diablo, con cabeza de chorlito y espaldas de ursus,
    con un moscardón zumbando en la calavera,
con mejillas empolvadas y manos enguantadas, que avanza con paso precipitado, y
    desesperado,
que entra y se sienta en el centro del redondel, haciendo señas aflictivas y se pone
    a llorar,
provocando un movimiento circular a expensas del gentío que, en efecto, se
    desborda tumultuosamente para rodear al afligido,

habiendo engendrado un redondel con cien redonditos gracias a otras muchas
  gentes que acaban de surgir de la nada y nada menos,
por obra de las señas aflictivas que hace el afligido antes que por eso mismo,
sino que todos los disfraces y los antifaces, y los capataces, incapaces y capaces lo
  rodean, todos los ropajes y los maquillajes y los personajes, con los homenajes
  y masajes de rigor,
los mortales y los inmortales, grandes y chicos, blancos y negros, mujeres y no
  mujeres, hombres y no hombres lo rodean,
involucrados y no involucrados en las señas que hace, mientras que hace las que
  no hace pero no hace, que no deshace pero que hace, sino que hace; y es lo que
  hace.

X

En las profundidades del mundo existen espacios muy grandes
—un vacío presidido por el propio vacío,
que es causa y origen del terror primordial, del pensamiento y del eco.
Existen honduras inimaginables, concavidades ante cuya fascinación, ante cuyo
  encantamiento,
seguramente uno se quedaría muerto.
Ruidos que seguramente uno desearía escuchar, formas y visiones que segura-
  mente uno desearía mirar,
cosas que seguramente uno desearía tocar, revelaciones que seguramente uno
  desearía conocer,
quién sabe con qué secreto deseo, de llegar a saber quién sabe qué.

En el ánima substancial, de la sincronía y de la duración del mundo,

que se interna en el abismo en que comenzó la creación del mundo, y que se

hunde en la médula del mundo,

se hace perceptible un olor, que podrás reconocer fácilmente, por no haber cono-

cido otro semejante;

el olor de verdad, el solo olor, el olor del abismo—y tendrás que conocerlo.

Pues tan sólo cuando hayas llegado a conocerlo te será posible comprender cómo

así era cierto que la sabiduría consiste en la falta de aire.

En la oscuridad profunda del mundo ha de darse la sabiduría; en los reinos her-

méticos del ánima;

en las vecindades del fuego y en el fuego mismo, en que el mismo fuego junto con

el aire es devorado por la oscuridad.

Y es por lo que nadie tiene idea del abismo, y por lo que nadie ha conocido el

abismo ni ha sentido el olor del abismo,

por lo que no se puede hablar de sabiduría entre los hombres, entre los vivos.

Mientras viva, el hombre no podrá comprender el mundo; el hombre ignora que

mientras no deje de vivir no será sabio.

Tiene aprensión por todo cuanto linda con lo sabio; en cuanto no puede com-

prender, ya desconfía

—no comprende otra cosa que no sea el vivir.

Y yo digo que uno debería procurar estar muerto.

Cueste lo que cueste, antes que morir. Uno tendría que hacer todo lo posible por estar muerto.

Las aguas te lo dicen—el fuego, el aire y la luz, con claro lenguaje.

Estar muerto.

El amor te lo dice, el mundo y las cosas todas, estar muerto.

La oscuridad nada dice. Es todo mutismo.

Hay que pensar en los espacios cerrados. En las bóvedas que se abren debajo de los mares.

En las cavernas, en las grutas—hay que pensar en las fisuras, en los antros interminables,

en las tinieblas.

Si piensas en ti, en alma y cuerpo, serás el mundo—en su interioridad y en sus formas visibles.

Acostúmbrate a pensar en una sola cosa; todo es oscuro.

Lo verdadero, lo real, lo existente; el ser y la esencia, es uno y oscuro.

Así la oscuridad es la ley del mundo; el fuego alienta la oscuridad y se apaga—es devorado por ésta.

Yo digo: es necesario pensar en el mundo—el interior del mundo me da en qué pensar. Soy oscuro.

No me interesa pensar en el mundo más allá de él; la luz es perturbadora, al igual que el vivir—tiene carácter transitorio.

Qué tendrá que ver el vivir con la vida; una cosa es el vivir, y la vida es otra cosa.

Vida y muerte son una y misma cosa.

XI

Una distancia recorrida, una ciudad deshabitada. En una ciudad perdida,
una ciudad habitada—nunca hubo tiempo.
El reflejo de la lluvia, una lluvia.
Un saludo, una seña—te saludan y se van.
Una música escuchada, un olvido—un olvido y no sé qué,
   un trance de inconsciencia,
   un olor,
   una mirada
   —qué recuerdo no se hunde, qué recuerdo no refluye.
   Y eso es todo.
   Nada ni nadie se queda; es uno mismo.
   Todo se queda con uno, y nada se queda
—la substancia, la tierra. Lo que no se toca, lo que se toca,
      lo que no hay,
      todo, es y se queda.
      Lo que ha sido, lo que es, lo que ha de ser, no hay tiempo
      —no hay nada—todo es.

No te duelas
   —no te duela nada.
   Nunca hubo tiempo; nunca ha sido nada; el humano todo lo tiene
   —cosa grave es la esperanza.
   Decir adiós y volverse adiós,
      es lo que cabe.

XII

Qué mano habrá sido tocada por esta mano.

Qué boca habrá sido besada por esta boca.

Qué ojos habrán sido mirados por estos ojos.

En medio de qué caminos, en medio de qué oscuridades, me habrán mirado estos ojos.

Dónde habrá sido encontrada esta mano por mi mano; cuándo habrá sido revelada esta mano por mi mano.

Qué día, qué hora, en qué lugar, habré encontrado este cuerpo y esta alma que amo.

En qué misterioso momento habré encontrado mi alma y mi cuerpo para amar como amo esta alma y este cuerpo que amo.

—■—

Este cuerpo, esta alma, están aquí.

Yo soy y estoy en esta alma, en este cuerpo, en esta alma que amo y en este cuerpo que amo.

Por el modo en que respiraba, en lo invisible y recóndito encontré esta alma.

En el modo de mirar y de ser de este cuerpo—en el modo de ser del ropaje, en el modo de estar y no estar, oscuro y sutil del ropaje, encontré el secreto, encontré el estar.

Con un ruido que resuena aquí, con una antigüedad muy remota,
    en esta distancia,
      cae la lluvia;
con un hálito de luces y de sombras, en que poco a poco se pierde este país
    ilusorio

—con un canto y con un pálpito,
con un sueño muy profundo, duerme este ser, en los resplandores de un limbo,
en los resplandores vacilantes de un limbo.

Desde muy lejanos sitios, desde muy hondos espacios,
con el soplo de júbilo en que el mundo se mece,
      llega un aire
—a la hora última en que llega este aire, cargado de presentimientos.
A la hora final del encantamiento, en que el mundo se hunde en algún lugar,
      más allá de la pared,
      en que yace este cuerpo que amo,
      en que yace esta alma que amo.

Más allá del más allá de todos los caminos,
      en que trasciende el olor de este cuerpo que amo,
      en que trasciende el olor de esta alma que amo.

De Visitante profundo (1964)

*Tu grave alegría discurre en un trance
de antigua navegación.*

*A mi madre y a mi tía Esther;
y a mis amigos muertos.*

I

Este visitante profundo habita en el vello y en las trompetas, decora una penumbra.

Vaga por los acordes y los perfiles diversos y aquí, en la ventana y allá, en el
    monte de la suprema finura,

este viajero me contempla, inexplicable,

se esconde en el olor claro y denso de las luminarias

y en aquellos tejidos que dibujó el olvido

—su mirada de piedra lisa y lavada

no suele posarse en el don de la vida,

sus ojos y aires y su bastón profundo cantan vapores nocturnos a las esferas grises

y mueven desde abajo y desde lo alto los flujos y los contornos de una broza de
    los sueños

que nuestro paso aplasta rítmicamente.

Una llamarada se cierne en las pláticas y ensombrece la borra de vino,

y anuncia la llegada de un muerto a los quehaceres matinales

—miedoso de la luz, el muerto de orejas de oro y cacao

tiene el tórax grabado en la memoria,

lágrimas tan hermosas como las arañas

y las manos dispuestas en su sitio,

entre la quietud de los salmos.

III

Del modo azul con que envuelves el mundo,
el modo azul en que lo amas.

Estoy entristecido, y enamorado de tu modo azul—del modo azul de estar que
 esperas a que yo pueda vivir y morir aquí en el mundo.
Del modo azul en que la idea te conduce al alba del gesto—percibes el estruendo
 que vives y lo explicas e interpretas a tus semejantes y a nosotros
en el borde del agua y el oído atento a las claras revelaciones de una trompeta
 transmutadora del deseo de la luz
en una llanura de vivas arenas y el latido al compás de la rueda que presagia la
 idea-niño y la primera y final virtud del suceso.
Del modo azul en que congregas tu pensamiento
—el modo azul dispuesto por ti en aquel esbozo lunar, cuando un día ofrendó el
 hombre su sonrisa al universo.

De anterior época a mi origen sólo conservo de ti el temor de nacer y hacer nacer,
 y el de estar muerto y que otros mueran o estén muertos,
porque—extraño caso de olvido—ya no sé de tu remota enseñanza.
Ya no sé de lo que me infundieras ni lo sabré, aun muerto;
es un extraño caso de olvido, modo azul,
y nos bambolearemos hasta que tus semejantes y nosotros y nuestros semejantes y
 tú pasemos a ti
con la sola semejanza para descifrarte viviendo y muriendo.

Cuando nos permitas a este bello mundo y a nosotros vulnerarte
y finjas tropezarte o estar dormido y simules haber sido visto o hagas entender
 que alguno vislumbró una partícula tuya
y con un relámpago enciendas el espanto y el asombro en nuestro mundo,
volveremos a mirar del animal, del muerto y del vivo y de la naturaleza de nues-
 tro mundo,
y nunca más olvidaremos. Será la redención, modo azul.

El músico y las escopetas, lo liviano, lo pesado y la sombra, los apodos, el algo-
dón y el calambre, el odio, los estafadores, la urraca, la edad y los candados, la
ortografía y el café y los mentirosos, la pulga y el marfil, el número, las abejas,
la visión y yo, la cola, el oro y las repisas y los achacosos,
esperamos la señal ansiosos por fundirnos y proseguir el diálogo contigo, modo
azul.

Que se alarguen los días y las noches sean humeantes y los moscardones tengan
una vida llevadera.
Que esto sea, y sea mucho más
—que el hombre deje de ser un protegido del animal y alcance lo humano, lo alto
y lo sencillo
—que la lana no le sea arrebatada al animal y se deje a cada cual estarse tran-
quilo.

Ahora se escucha un grito, proferido quién sabe por qué;
no es grito de hombre ni tampoco es de animal, pero es un grito de cosa
—su origen se halla aquí, y parece ser inadmisible
—modo azul, yo estoy entristecido y perplejo por siempre.
Es mi intención dejar de verme y no saber nada de mí, y me comeré, si no pu-
dieras hacer por ser visto.

V

Como el día alimenta unos sueños estériles y lastima tu naturaleza angelical,
has de partir en pos de la noche

—y yo te diré que ella suele pedir, como un mendigo, toda la vida:
raramente se conmueve.
Pero tú, con tu tierna manera increíble,
eres comunicativo y la conmoverás en aquella claraboya, si le dices:
"Quiero la muerte, pero no morir"
—y los que descansan alejados del fuego, escucharán la palabra estremecida de tu
vuelo
y no querrán saber que están muertos al ver que te habrían amado.
Y de tal modo conocerás las imaginaciones de la noche
y lo indecible de muerte en tu forma,
el júbilo mío: estoy de pie y con un fuego en las manos.

(De noche tu ropaje con unos vivos de color blanco refleja una música de ciu-
dades y de soles y deja mirar un otro, denso ropaje que hace vibrar los puentes
y ocurrir los viajes, y hace que se quede la noche en tus ojos.)

VI

Bajo una tiniebla conduce el dolor la antigua dinámica con que evocas la fragancia
de los vegetales
—en los resplandores que el corazón elevará de las montañas y en el olvido de las
grandes campanas
—en los polos dilatados y endurecidos de las canciones está el acorde central que
te detiene a contemplar las alas excesivas de los habitantes:
relacionas la cadencia de tus dedos con la vaga ascensión del humo cuando ha per-
dido un polo su virtud.

Bajo lo solo, a la hora de lo perplejo y de lo admirable, cae la tarde;
lleva tu peso el horizonte hacia las traslaciones y hacia las profundidades
y el muerto es cálido, mundial en las espumas, en los murmullos y en la luz
—y entra el agua en ebullición, ronda la profecía.

Se proyecta en las grutas, y en tus labios y en tus sueños no fenece la tensión,
un badajo te aparta de la camisola nocturna;
yo no pereceré sino cuando pongas un huevo en testimonio inmortal de la tensión.

VII

Vive a la vera del lenguaje, la cabeza flotante en un cuerpo que no hay
un dedo en la neblina
el agua corriente en el mundo de los que agracian su estar con un borde de lino
y otro dedo en el viento que mece los soles del milagro nombrado por el verano y
    la lluvia
y ancianidad de la luz que todavía no viste
una noche otro dedo paralelo a una ambigua melodía en el puente
y el peso del llanto en el ramillete guardado generación tras generación
cuando las modulaciones y la furia del agua fija y reluciente pasan de largo
mas el vínculo te llama y te llama y toca y toca tu corazón otro dedo con el apoyo
    del fuego
—parpadeas a poco la fórmula mágica que ronda tu cuerpo y lame la áspera vida
—a una ciudad vas, y tiene apagado el mechero alguien que está y está por nacer
y le comes su intención y un fondo de tambor se descencanta ante ti.
La fibra y los ruidos difundidos en el interior de la tierra, algo hallan en ti de su
    secreto original

y llega conquistadora la medida de las presiones en los rumores nocturnos
cabe decir que el molino creció y las vidas renacieron anteriores a las nubes,
expulsa tu figura, acoge la verdadera y volarás a mirar el fondo del agua
—cada mayo, cada instante y cada año cabe decir si el agua verdadera se oculta,
si el fuego se oculta y te quema
—y en tanto,
apresura la expulsión de tu figura porque todo está expulsándose.

Hay ciudades ocultas que guardan ciudades en el corazón y el primer día su re-
    splandor subyuga, y el último es un olvido que brilla en el ojo del hombre
—sus calles disciernen el mundo y evocan la cumbre, y la voluta olorece a
    cabellos y a calavera
—de ti a mí, de ellos a ellos, de todos a todos va y viene la voluta, y en la ciudad
    se esparce;
lava tu frente una lluvia concisa la vez que suspiras, y el trazo del péndulo y las
    húmedas fuentes, a ti te devuelven el rastro de la marina y lisa clave de los sueños.

De todo pálpito te libera el edificio del eco;
tu grave alegría discurre en un trance de antigua navegación.
Una mano petrificadora en tus mejillas, y la ansiedad, y la epístola y los minerales,
tocan una música para los animales afectuosos que nombran tu ropaje a la caden-
    cia de tu risa y de tu llanto
—y tus cabellos te conducen a la ausencia.

Y en aquellas ciudades—¡oh, habitante!—la muerte es fuerte y diversa, y pode-
    rosa la agonía; los sueños manan de tu sangre

—revelan el astro de la letra olvidada—la letra que falta a la palabra que falta
—y se desborda el lujo de la sangre, en unas ciudades donde no se puede morir.

VIII

Evocan las aguas un canto para helar el vaho y la sombra.
Que tu cabeza lavada alargue hacia aquí la medida y escudriñaré los costados del
    mar
y la perdida alumbre que brilla en la orgullosa humedad muerta.

(En la lejanía del abismo, de pronto la mariposa nocturna se volvió contemplativa,
    invisible y paciente como la devoción y flexibilidad que se le volaban por las
    patas.)
Uno llega, se oculta por no saber que ha llegado y se encuentra un estruendo:
se diría tu voz,
pero la incidencia de la luz y un olor de vejez
no dejan ver su trance original, que era una sonrisa.

X

Yo te veo
—un destello me acoge si los orígenes de la noche se han vertido.
En cuanto cruzas la negrura, un soplo del corno te borra;
eres la significación irremediable de las ciudades y de los resplandores.

Estás en las dos orillas, en mí; en el lejano tejido habitas el humo y la colina
y la textura de la lluvia se asemeja a lo que deshabitas y a lo que no habitaré.
Te busco en mi dolor cuando mi dolor por sí solo existía
—cuando yo era un soplo y una arena,
dónde, en qué estabas,
eres en ti pero en realidad no serías.

A que te trueque en fuente me instas melancólicamente, maga de medias negras
tal vez amante del olvido
—habitante que sabe que no existe y que no elude el verse y el sentirse:
hay humor en que sí yo sea y que tú no.
Sería asombroso el que sin mí vivieses.

Esté tu voz; esté por siempre aquí,
así fuera que yo la escuchase o que no.
Esté, siempre esté.

XI

De la altura del muerto que mira los trances del crepúsculo
ha quedado en ti una lejana chispa
—el trazo de la forma azul en el fuerte acorde que mece el viento con una lejana
chispa,
en ti está.

El silencio eleve un poco de dulzura y se aparte del olvido
para morir en algún olvido,
y se diluya contigo y fenezca al fluír de la lluvia;
y que todo sea lenguaje en formación a la señal de un suspiro.
Y una nave de los cielos descubra nuestra carne y nuestro dolor.

XVI

No toques esa música
—cuando hace frío, necesitan de tu gracia un hálito las formas, un silbido y un
rocío.

Es húmedo el abismo de tu peso y las esfinges no te contemplan,
las contemplas tú por ser esfinge, si el ámbito es tuyo y te restriega
—el ámbito espectador de lo tuyo en el principio y término de tu vida sinfónica.

Deseo indagar qué viento te lleva y qué lluvia, y la esencia de tu mirar en el país
de las causas
—te insto a que vengas y me despiertes, y me maravilles.
Me apremia el tránsito de la noche, y me desune;
mi cuerpo se distribuye, y nadie llega a verlo ni a verme.
Me acuesto—si suspiro o me toco o miro, todo acabaría: la esperanza de la
transparencia,

la vida propiamente dicha; la promesa de cabellos y de luces de tu aparición
y la hospitalidad de los templos y la acogida de las canciones.

Mi voz aclama una proeza, escribe el rabioso ademán de la mano negra que tu
    profesión es inútil.
Si no identificas tu futuro con los peces—si no te transformas,
caerá en las aguas la mucha música de los negros, y discurrirá la ciudad en un
    silbido.

XVII

Hunde los labios en la muerte colectiva al amparo de los dedos arriba y abajo
sepúltate en lo no argumentado ni dicho y en el fleco a la luz de los que mueren
    de vacilación
—si viene la muerte no solamente de la vida, sino por vacilar.
(La muerte suma y armónica nada tiene que ver con la muerte por vacilación,
y no digo que quien no vacila fuese inmortal.)

Si no percibes el olor de una araña y no sabes lo que dice lo inmóvil, entonces
    mueres;
pero nunca si tu frente se mordiese, siempre que mientras tanto no soñaras que
    ella te mordía.
Cuando no tú vacilación, la muerte espera el mordisco de tu frente para recibirte.

Mas, me lleva el amor a clamar por tu conservación en ecos lucientes y en tareas
    universales,

en masas activas e inertes, que hielen y den júbilo.

Frenético clamor suscita tu conservación, tu tiempo particular sin noticia de temperatura.

Sea inscrito mi deseo en la gravedad, en el calor y en la redondez.

Como una luz

Llegada la hora en que el astro se apague
quedarán mis ojos en los aires que contigo fulguraban.
Silenciosamente y como una luz
reposa en mi camino
la transparencia del olvido.

Tu aliento me devuelve a la espera y a la tristeza de la tierra,
no te apartes del caer de la tarde
—no me dejes descubrir sino detrás de ti
lo que tengo todavía que morir.

Eres visible

Permaneces todo el tiempo en el olor de las montañas
cuando el sol se retira,
y me parece escuchar tu respiración en la frescura de la sombra
como un adiós pensativo.

De tu partida, que es como una lumbre, se condolerán estas claras imágenes
por el viento de la tarde mecidas aquí y a lo lejos;
yo te acompaño, con el rumor de las hojas, miro por ti las cosas que amabas
—el alba no borrará tu paso, eres visible.

A ti

Al calor de tu forma progresa mi sangre, en el aire de sueño
el clima para lo solo eres tú
—una sombra canta para ti en el fondo del agua al compás de mi corazón
y en tu mirar mis ojos están silenciosos por la música
al soplo de la luz,
en el cielo y en la oscuridad.

Esta noche reuno tu forma,
el eco de tu boca en medio de una olvidada canción
—y te doy un abrazo.

Ven

Ven; yo vivo de tu dibujo
y de tu perfumada melodía,
soñé en la estrella a que con un canto se podría llegar
—te vi aparecer y no pude asirte, a turbadora distancia te llevaba el canto

y era mucha lejanía y poco tu aliento para alcanzar a tiempo un fulgor de mi
   corazón
—el que ahora estalla ahogado por alguna lluvia compasiva.

Ven, sin embargo; deja que mi mano imprima inolvidable fuerza a tu olvido,
acércate a mirar mi sombra en la pared,
ven una vez; quiero cumplir mi deseo de adiós.

The Saenz Effect

An Afterword by Leonardo García-Pabón

Timeless image,
Eternal and always fresh,
Even this is an image.
Like the days, the nights.
An event, without beginning or end.

Jaime Saenz

On the night of Jaime Saenz's wake in August 1986, three friends, those closest and most loyal to his work, and a drunk acquaintance of Jaime's who had fallen asleep in a chair, stayed late to keep his body (and perhaps his soul) company. As we bid farewell, we imagined that he had finally arrived at the "state of death" that he always heralded as a path to true knowledge. To ease our loss, we spent the night reading aloud fragments of his writings. I bring up this moment because it seems to have presaged the way many people currently experience Saenz's work. Small groups of those familiar with his life and immensely loyal to his literature, in some cases friends and life companions, in other cases strangers only recently fallen under his spell, come together to read

Saenz, to cultivate the beauty and profundity of his writing.

It would also seem that Saenz's work is, indeed, preceded by an image. A writer's image is sometimes confused with his work. It's a phenomenon not infrequent in world literature, though less frequent in Bolivia. During his life, Saenz fostered, whether intentionally or not, an image of himself that attracted and repelled people with equal intensity. As a writer, an alcoholic, and a rebel in the provincial society of La Paz in the 1940s and 1950s, Saenz was perceived as extravagant, to say the least, and his work was sometimes dismissed as the product of delirium. Moreover, by effectively breaking with literary norms, Saenz's poetry, and later his prose, began to attract all kinds of attention. The poetry unwinds in long lines marked by labyrinthine relationships, speculations on the poetic subject's otherness, and sharp linguistic paradoxes that border on nonsense. It does not offer itself to those looking for an easy and comfortable read. On the other hand, his prose dared to reveal the most hidden, perhaps darkest, but always most human sides of a Bolivian society still entangled in colonial structures. His work addresses and celebrates social groups that the dominant Westernized elites refused—and largely still continue to refuse—to see: alcoholics, homosexuals, the homeless, poor artisans, the indigenous Aymara. Nonetheless, an extraordinary phenomenon emerged in the 1960s: His writings began to enjoy immense popularity among young artists and writers of the time. In his room in an old factory building, he received friends, and ideas and literary works flowered in what he called "Krupp workshops." Not just anybody was invited to these gatherings; one had to be accepted by Saenz. These workshop groups gained a reputation for being hermetic and somewhat esoteric. In reality, they consisted of literary friends bonded by Saenz's strong personality, with a wild enthusiasm for poetry and art. Saenz used to say that in matters of art one had to be fanatical, but not dumbfounded by fanaticism.

If something has lasted after Saenz's death, it is precisely this devoted enthusiasm for his work. Small groups of loyal admirers continue reading and reflecting on Saenz's writings. Interestingly, these companies of enthusiasts have proliferated far apart and almost unknown to one another. In a process that the French philosopher Gilles Deleuze would call "rhizomatic" (growing through bifurcation, laterally and without predictable direction), new clusters of Saenz's readers have been appearing not only throughout Bolivia but also throughout all Latin America, many European countries, and now the United States. The propagation of his work is not sustained by publishers or government institutions (despite the fact that Saenz is considered one of the great Bolivian writers) but rather by readers in love with his language, those who by some chance have come upon his work. In addition to increasing commentary and criticism, there are seminars in Colombia, editions of his poems in Chile, translations of his poetry and prose into Italian, and now English versions of some of his loveliest books. In Bolivia, Saenz's mark is surprising: His work has been treated by filmmakers, dramatists, painters, journalists, and intellectuals. Ever larger groups among the very young have absorbed Saenz's poetry as an integral part of their soul-making.

This is what I would like to call the "Saenz effect." As with his life, if you come close to his literature, you run the risk of being seduced forever. Then, either you are a Saenzian or you aren't. Once drawn into his particular vision of the city of La Paz, his characters, and his meditations on death, it is difficult to relinquish his fascinating vision of the world. As with the work of all great writers, his generates a universe in and of itself, with its own times, laws, rites, and labyrinths. In the case of Saenz, that universe is modeled on a profound and singular vision of Bolivian (and Latin American) urban society, a complex and existential vision that has few counterparts in other Spanish literatures.

As the epigraph that begins this afterword indicates, Saenz was and is an image. His work, too, is a marvelous image that proposes Bolivian and Latin American reality better than a thousand studies. His writing continues to be "eternal and always fresh," "an event without beginning or end." It is a magnet of meanings drawing enlightened, fervent readers across the borders of language.

March 29, 2000

Designer: Sandy Drooker
Compositor: Binghamton Valley Composition
Text: 9/12 Fournier
Display: Akzidenz Grotesk, Fournier
Printer and binder: Thomson-Shore, Inc.